# LINCOLN'S FLYING SPIES

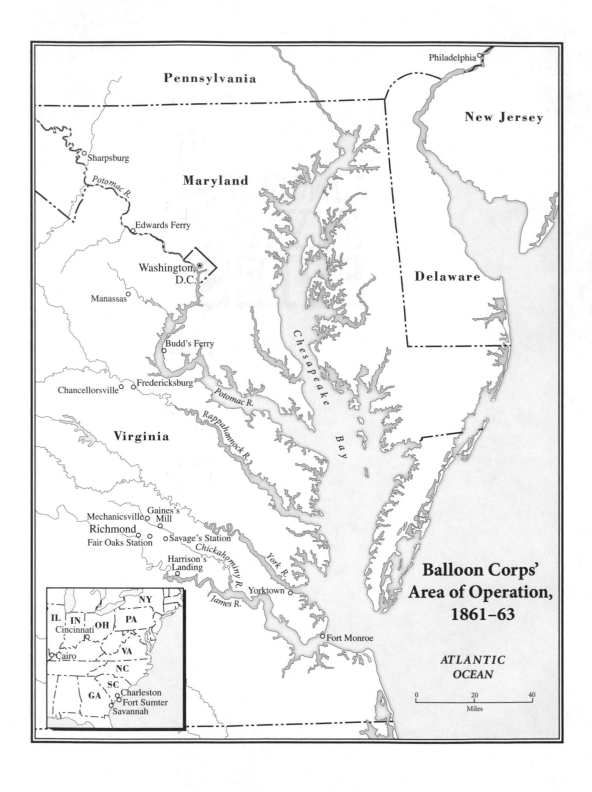

Pennsylvania

Philadelphia

New Jersey

Sharpsburg

*Potomac R.*

Maryland

Edwards Ferry

Washington, ⊛
D.C.

Delaware

Manassas

Budd's Ferry

Chesapeake
Bay

Chancellorsville

Fredericksburg

*Potomac R.*

*Rappahannock R.*

Virginia

Gaines's
Mill

Mechanicsville

Richmond

Savage's Station

Fair Oaks Station

*Chickahominy R.*

Harrison's
Landing

York R.

Yorktown

*James R.*

Fort Monroe

Balloon Corps'
Area of Operation,
1861–63

*ATLANTIC
OCEAN*

NY

IL IN OH PA
Cincinnati

VA

Cairo

NC

SC

GA Charleston
Fort Sumter
Savannah

0        20        40
Miles

# LINCOLN'S FLYING SPIES

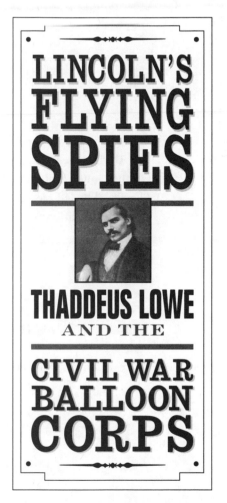

## THADDEUS LOWE

### AND THE

## CIVIL WAR BALLOON CORPS

## GAIL JARROW

CALKINS CREEK
*Honesdale, Pennsylvania*

ISBN: 978-1-59078-719-9

Library of Congress Control Number: 2010925627

Map, page 2, by Mapping Specialists Ltd., Madison, Wisconsin

CALKINS CREEK
An Imprint of Boyds Mills Press, Inc.
815 Church Street
Honesdale, Pennsylvania 18431

10 9 8 7 6 5 4 3 2 1

For Robert, who still remembered—after forty years—the Civil War balloon in Jules Verne's *The Mysterious Island*

—G.J.

# Contents

**Lowe Takes Off**
Thaddeus Lowe goes up in the balloon *Intrepid* to spy on Confederate army positions in Virginia. The sides of the basket in which he stands are only about as high as his knees. A balloon crew of Union soldiers holds three ropes so that the balloon does not break free. The photograph was taken in spring 1862, probably by Civil War photographer James Gibson.

CHAPTER ONE

# Eye in the Sky

Aeronaut Thaddeus Lowe dangled under a giant silk balloon decorated with George Washington's portrait. On the ground several hundred feet below him, three dozen Union soldiers held the three ropes that kept Lowe and the balloon from drifting over Confederate territory.

From the wicker basket in which he stood, Lowe looked down on white tents in the Union camps. The nearby Chickahominy River, swollen by weeks of rain, snaked across the Virginia peninsula. Lowe surveyed the landscape of green pastures, leafy treetops, dense swamps, muddy roads, and farmhouse roofs.

On this May afternoon in 1862, the sky was clear enough for Lowe to see six miles away into the Confederate capital of Richmond. Using his spyglass, he spotted church spires, the white capitol building, and people on the streets.

Lowe noted the earthworks fortifying the city. Rebel soldiers, their faces turned toward the sky, ran under the cover of trees so that the aeronaut would not be able to count their numbers. But they could not hide their tents and campfires from the Union balloon.

On the west side of the city, Lowe watched a train moving into Richmond. He guessed it was filled with weapons and men. The Confederates were strengthening the capital's defenses to protect it against a hundred thousand Union soldiers poised to attack from the east.

Suddenly, Lowe noticed a puff of white smoke from a line of trees. A second later, he heard the explosive bang of a cannon. Before he could react, the cannon's shell screamed past his balloon, barely missing it. Lowe tracked the shell as it crashed into a field and exploded.

He shouted down to the men holding the ropes, "Haul in the cables—quick!"

At that moment, a second shell whizzed through the balloon rigging and burst in the air.

His ears ringing from the bang, Lowe yelled, "Are you pulling in there, you men?"

He heard another bang followed by a shell shrieking past. A second Confederate battery had started firing at him!

Before the shells could strike the balloon, Lowe's ground crew yanked it safely out of artillery range behind the cover of a hill. Once again, Thaddeus Lowe had escaped the Rebel cannons.

For two years during the Civil War, the Balloon Corps spied on the Confederate army. The Rebels tried to shoot down the eye in the sky. They never succeeded. The balloons survived Confederate guns, harsh weather, and raging battles.

Starting in the summer of 1861, Thaddeus Lowe and his fellow aeronauts provided Union generals with information about the enemy. They counted troops, directed artillery fire, created maps, and calmed the panicked citizens of Washington. By the time they were finally grounded in 1863 by their own army's bureaucracy, the Civil War balloonists had become the nation's first air force.

**Thaddeus Lowe, Balloon Spy**
During the Civil War, Thaddeus Lowe was employed as a civilian by the Union army and did not wear a uniform. Lowe typically wore high riding boots and a long coat. He holds a dark hat similar to what military field officers wore. A rolled-up map is in his left hand. On his side hangs the spyglass he used for balloon observations.

CHAPTER TWO

# Following the Clouds

Thaddeus Sobieski Constantine Lowe was already a famous aeronaut by the time the Civil War broke out in April 1861. The handsome young man was skilled at attracting attention. Newspapers and magazines had been covering his balloon adventures for several years.

Lowe had come a long way from the White Mountains of New Hampshire, where he was born on August 20, 1832. Growing up as the son of a farmer and storekeeper, Thaddeus became interested in science, especially chemistry and mechanics. But as one of a dozen Lowe children in rural Jefferson, he went to school only a few months a year.

When he was fourteen, Thaddeus moved to Massachusetts to join his older brother and learn a trade. In a town near Boston, Thaddeus worked as an apprentice to a boot maker, studying science on his own.

One night, he performed his first flying experiment, using a black cat as the passenger. Thaddeus placed the cat in a cage, which he tied to the end of a large kite. As he and his friends let out the rope, the wind off the Atlantic Ocean caught the kite, taking it up a thousand feet. When the boys brought down the kite, the frightened cat bolted, never to be seen again. That was the last time Thaddeus used an animal in his experiments.

Instead, he vowed to build a flying machine that would take *him* into the clouds. He knew his dream required money and knowledge, and he set out to get both. "I saved every dollar I made," Lowe wrote later, "read all the scientific books I could obtain—courted the society of men who knew something—and tried in every way to store my mind with knowledge. ..."

## The French Are First

The first balloon passengers were three French animals—a sheep, rooster, and duck. They took their brief voyage on September 19, 1783, in a hot air balloon developed by the Montgolfier brothers. A hot air balloon rises because the heated air inside the balloon is lighter than the cooler air outside.

Two months later, the first humans flew when Jean-François Pilâtre de Rozier and François Laurent, the marquis d'Arlandes, drifted five miles over Paris in a Montgolfier hot air balloon. That same year, French scientist Jacques Charles invented the hydrogen balloon. In this French print, Charles and a companion take off from Paris on the first untethered flight of a hydrogen balloon, December 1, 1783.

America did not see a free flight until January 1793 when Jean-Pierre Blanchard, accompanied by his friend's small dog, launched from Philadelphia in a hydrogen balloon.

When he was eighteen, Thaddeus attended a chemistry demonstration by a traveling lecturer. These demonstrations were a type of entertainment, and the lecturers were called "professor," though they lacked a university education. The professor asked the audience for an assistant, and an eager Thaddeus volunteered. He performed so well that the professor invited him to join the lecture tour.

For two years, Thaddeus traveled with the professor as his assistant. He learned all he could about chemistry and developed his showmanship skills. At age twenty, he went out alone on the lecture circuit as Professor of Chemistry T. S. C. Lowe. Soon he was earning enough to support himself and his new wife, Leontine.

### AN AERONAUT DREAM

Thaddeus didn't give up his dream of flying. Experimenting with small hydrogen balloons, he learned more about air currents. He studied the work of John Wise, America's greatest living aeronaut.

During the nineteenth century, many balloonists made money by staging public balloon ascents and charging people to watch. Lowe saw a business opportunity. By 1856, twenty-four-year-old

**Lowe Over Ottawa, Canada, 1858**
Thaddeus Lowe's balloon flights in Canada during the summer of 1858 brought him attention and publicity for the first time, even though he had made several ascensions during the previous two years.

**Leontine Augustine Gachon Lowe**
In 1855, Thaddeus met his wife in New York City at one of his lectures. He married her a week later. The French-born Leontine shared his enthusiasm for science. The couple was married for fifty-seven years and had ten children. Lowe later wrote that meeting her was "the greatest and best thing that ever happened to me. ..."

**Professor Thaddeus S. C. Lowe, Age Twenty-Two**
Lowe was over six feet tall, had blue eyes, thick black hair, and an auburn mustache.

## Father of Nineteeth-Century Ballooning

John Wise was born in Lancaster, Pennsylvania, on February 24, 1808. As a young man, he built pianos and cabinets. He soon gave up woodworking to follow his dream of becoming a professional balloonist. Wise called his first balloon flight "one of the happiest moments I ever experienced in my life. ..."

Wise was the most famous American aeronaut of his time. Despite making hundreds of flights, however, he was more interested in science than adventure. He studied weather patterns, air pressure, and currents, and he developed improvements in constructing and flying balloons. In an 1850 book, Wise explained how to make, inflate, and sail balloons. This book became the manual for young aeronauts like Thaddeus Lowe.

After more than forty years of flying, Wise disappeared in 1879 during a doomed balloon flight over Lake Michigan. His body was never found.

Thaddeus had saved enough cash from lecturing to buy his own balloon, and he began giving balloon rides to paying customers. Next he set up a factory in Hoboken, New Jersey, near New York City, to build balloons for other aeronauts.

But Thaddeus had even bigger plans. He remembered watching the sky as a boy. "I had often seen ... the clouds moving in different directions," he wrote later, "the higher ones going east and the lower ones west, and it occurred to me that once in this upper current, I could sail across the Atlantic and land on the continent of Europe."

In the mid-nineteenth century, the fastest way to travel across the Atlantic Ocean was by steamship. The three-thousand-mile trip took at least nine days. Thaddeus was convinced a balloon could do it in three.

No aeronaut had ever accomplished this, although a few had the same idea. As early as 1843, John Wise announced his plan to make the voyage, but he couldn't raise money to pay for it. In spring 1859, he and Lowe exchanged letters about building such a balloon together. Wise went into partnership with others, however, and Thaddeus decided to build his airship alone.

## AMERICA'S BIGGEST BALLOON

Lowe realized that the balloon's gas would gradually leak out as he crossed the Atlantic. So he designed a mammoth balloon that held enough gas to keep him aloft for several days. By September 1859, after three months of work, his employees in the Hoboken factory finished the *City of New York*. It was the largest balloon in America at the time— two hundred feet high from the top of its envelope, or gas bag, to the bottom of the lifeboat underneath.

To pay for his project, Lowe displayed the balloon in a New York City park and charged twenty-five cents admission. For several weeks, thousands of people flocked to see it, and Thaddeus received national publicity. He told reporters that his Atlantic crossing would increase scientific knowledge and prove that ballooning was a safe way to travel.

When he was ready to launch, Lowe had an unexpected setback. New York City's gas works could not pump coal gas into his balloon fast enough to inflate it.

Leaders in Philadelphia, Pennsylvania, were eager to show that *their* city could produce enough gas. They paid for Lowe to move his operations there. He changed the balloon's name to the *Great Western* and waited for the end of stormy

**The *City of New York***
This drawing appeared in *Frank Leslie's Illustrated Newspaper* in November 1859. The giant muslin-cotton balloon was 130 feet across when fully inflated. Lowe planned to equip the basket with canvas walls and ceiling, a stove, and even carrier doves to send regular updates to the press. A 30-foot-long lifeboat, named *Leontine*, after Lowe's wife, hangs below the basket. A trapdoor in the bottom of the basket allowed the crew to climb into the boat in case of an ocean landing. The boat had an engine, sails, a waterproof rubber cover, and six months of supplies for a crew of ten. Despite the scene shown, the balloon never got off the ground in New York.

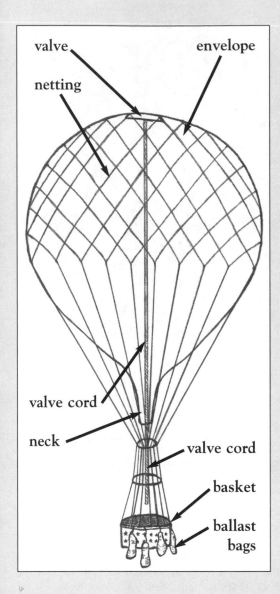

valve

netting

envelope

valve cord

neck

valve cord

basket

ballast bags

# How Lowe's Hydrogen Balloon Worked

Balloon passengers traveled in a wicker basket attached by ropes to the gas bag, or envelope. The envelope was filled with hydrogen, a gas that rises because it is lighter than air. Hydrogen is flammable, and aeronauts avoided balloon explosions by keeping fire and sparks away from the gas.

When Thaddeus Lowe used his balloons on the battlefield, he produced hydrogen using a chemical process. When he was near a city, he inflated the balloons with hydrogen-containing coal gas. City gas works throughout the United States heated coal to make the gas, which was piped to homes to use for lighting. Coal gas was not as light as pure hydrogen, and it had a foul smell. But it was cheaper.

Lowe built a balloon envelope by sewing together sections of cloth—either cotton muslin or silk, which was sturdier material. The bottom of the envelope had an open neck where Lowe added the gas. A yellowish varnish coating protected the envelope from weather and sealed the fabric so that gas seeped out more slowly. Netting surrounded the envelope for support.

Lowe could not steer his balloon. By controlling the balloon's up-and-down motion, however, he could search for a wind current that would carry the balloon in the general direction he wanted to travel.

To take the balloon lower, he released some gas through the valve at the top of the envelope. A long cord, which was connected to the valve, dropped through the envelope and out its neck. When Lowe pulled the cord, the valve opened and the gas escaped. When he let go of the cord, springs closed the valve door.

To make the balloon rise, the aeronaut lightened the load. Lowe carried bags of sand to use as ballast. By dropping sand overboard, he could send the balloon higher.

Lowe used several instruments as he flew, including a compass and thermometer. A barometer, which measures air pressure, helped him figure out how high he was flying, because air pressure decreases as a balloon rises.

When Lowe was ready to land, he gradually released the envelope's gas through the valve until the balloon approached the ground. If he spotted people below, he called to them—sometimes with a megaphone—so that they grabbed the rope hanging below the basket.

**Inflating the *Great Western*, 1860**
Lowe (in center foreground wearing tall black hat) moved his huge balloon to Philadelphia, renamed it the *Great Western*, and put it on public display. The new name was based on the largest steamship of the time, the *Great Eastern*, which crossed the Atlantic Ocean from Great Britain to the United States in June 1860. During the Civil War, Lowe cut up the *Great Western's* envelope and used the pieces for ground cloths to protect other balloons during their inflation.

winter and spring weather over the Atlantic.

During the summer of 1860, he made at least one successful test flight in the *Great Western*. But in September while the balloon was being inflated during a strong wind, it burst. Lowe would have to make a new envelope for his Atlantic crossing.

Before paying for another balloon, Lowe's Philadelphia sponsors wanted to be sure that his theory about an east-flowing air current was correct. What if the balloon had no chance of reaching Europe? They asked the opinion of Professor Joseph Henry, a respected scientist and head of the Smithsonian Institution in Washington.

Henry responded that if the balloon were big enough, held the gas long enough, and stayed high enough, it would be carried east across the Atlantic. But he added, "I would not … advise that the first experiment of this character be made across the ocean. …"

**Lowe the Showman**
Thaddeus Lowe, age twenty-eight, is shown in a photograph that appeared on tickets for his 1860 transatlantic balloon launch.

## TEST FLIGHT

Acting quickly on Professor Henry's advice, Lowe headed to Cincinnati, Ohio, to make a test flight over land. He planned to use one of his other balloons, the *Enterprise*.

Thaddeus contacted Murat Halstead, the editor of one of the city's newspapers, who arranged for him to lecture about his balloon work. As an experienced showman, Lowe raised both money and public enthusiasm for his flight.

He set up the *Enterprise* on a Cincinnati vacant lot and waited for the right weather conditions. On the night of April 19, 1861, while he was the guest of honor at a banquet, Thaddeus got word that the winds were perfect. Still wearing his tall silk hat and long formal coat, he hurried to his balloon. He took along a large revolver, "thinking [he] might possibly have occasion to use it." Editor Halstead collected food from the banquet table and a pile of newly printed newspapers and tossed everything into the basket of the *Enterprise*.

In the early morning hours of April 20, under a bright moon, Lowe and the *Enterprise* lifted off. At first, the wind near the ground blew the balloon toward the west. Then just as Lowe predicted, when the balloon reached seven thousand feet, it entered an eastward air current.

As Lowe drifted toward the east, the sun rose and heated the balloon's gas. The expanding gas lifted the *Enterprise* to a height of more than three miles. Using his spyglass, a handheld telescope, Thaddeus scanned the fields and woods below. He had no way of knowing exactly where he was. When he noticed men in a field, he lowered the balloon by releasing some gas.

"What state is this?" he called to them.

The startled men shouted, "Virginia." When they realized the voice had come from a huge balloon above their heads, the terrified workers ran into the woods.

Lowe poured out some sand from a ballast bag, and the balloon rose again. As he crossed the Blue Ridge Mountains, the temperature dropped below zero. Wrapping his coat and blankets around him, he shivered and watched the food in his basket freeze solid.

Finally, changing winds took the *Enterprise* southward, and Thaddeus spotted the blue line of the Atlantic Ocean. His flight had been a success. He had flown on an eastward wind for more than six hundred miles to the coast. The flight had taken about nine hours. Now he was convinced he could cross the Atlantic in two days.

**Inflation in Cincinnati**
Lowe's inflated *Enterprise* is surrounded by a crowd in Cincinnati, Ohio, in April 1861. The balloon could hold twenty thousand cubic feet of gas. Lowe flew to South Carolina on the high eastward air currents, known today as the jet stream.

## ROUGH LANDING

Thaddeus searched for a safe place to land his balloon. Unfortunately, he picked the wrong place at the wrong time—South Carolina.

Four months before, South Carolina had become the first of eleven Southern states to break away from the United States and form the Confederate States of America. For years, the South and North had argued over the issue of slavery. The last straw for Southerners was the November 1860 presidential election of Abraham Lincoln, who opposed allowing slavery in the new western territories. Only eight days before Lowe landed in South Carolina's farmlands, the state fired cannons at United States troops inside the federal garrison of Fort Sumter in Charleston Harbor. The Civil War had begun.

Once on the ground, Lowe opened the valve and released all of the gas. He folded up the empty envelope and stowed it in the basket. When the local people saw Thaddeus's pistol and the Ohio newspapers he carried, they figured he was a Yankee. They called for him to be "shot on the spot where he had dropped from the skies."

Talking fast and using his charm, Lowe instead persuaded the suspicious group to take him and his balloon to the county seat. There, he caught a train for the South

**Sumter Cannon**
Union soldiers defend Fort Sumter against the Confederate bombardment on April 12, 1861. During the nineteenth century, a New York City company owned by Nathaniel Currier (1813–1888) and James Merritt Ives (1824–1895) published popular prints like this one. Currier and Ives scenes were created after the event and were neither eyewitness drawings nor necessarily accurate.

Carolina capital of Columbia, hoping he could find a northbound train.

He didn't get far. When Thaddeus stepped off the train in Columbia, he was shocked to find that word had spread about him. An angry crowd called for him to be hanged as a spy. The sheriff arrested Lowe at gunpoint and took him to the jail. Thaddeus became one of the Confederates' first Yankee prisoners.

Lowe's fame and reputation saved him. The president of the nearby college had heard of his work and explained to the sheriff that the balloon trip was strictly scientific. No one—including Thaddeus Lowe—knew that within three months, the aeronaut *would* become a Union spy.

Released from jail, Lowe boarded a train for Cincinnati. During his four-day trip, he met nervous Northerners leaving the hostile South. He saw armed Confederate soldiers on their way to Virginia to fight. By the time he arrived in Ohio, he was "fully convinced the country was facing a severe struggle. ..."

Everything changed for Thaddeus Lowe. Crossing the Atlantic no longer seemed as important as serving his country. And he knew exactly how his balloons could help the Union army.

**Fort Sumter After Surrender**
The Confederate flag flies over Fort Sumter in Charleston, South Carolina, three days after the Rebels' attack started the Civil War. Southern photographer Alma Pelot took this photograph inside the damaged fort after Union soldiers had surrendered.

## First Transatlantic Balloon Crossing

Balloonists did not succeed in crossing the Atlantic until August 1978, nearly 120 years after Lowe's planned attempt. Three American balloonists in the helium-filled *Double Eagle II* made the trip in just less than six days. This monument of the balloon stands in Presque Isle, Maine, the launch site for the transatlantic crossing.

CHAPTER THREE

# Aeronaut Over Washington

Thaddeus Lowe believed that balloons were the perfect way to spy on Confederate forces, working better than scouts or lookout towers. He was determined to persuade government and military leaders that the army needed a balloon corps and that *he* should be its leader.

In early June 1861, Thaddeus packed up the *Enterprise* and headed from his home in Philadelphia to Washington. When he arrived, he found a city full of Northern soldiers. Immediately after the attack on Fort Sumter two months before, President Abraham Lincoln had called for the Northern states to send troops to put down the Southern rebellion. Tens of thousands of enthusiastic men enlisted.

"We had been attacked and our Flag captured," said one New Hampshire soldier. "There was absolutely no other alternative left us—we must fight in self-defense, or cowardly surrender."

Meanwhile, twenty thousand Confederate troops had gathered in Manassas, Virginia, just twenty-five miles southwest of Washington. Newspapers in both the North and South urged attack. Many Yankee and Rebel soldiers were eager to fight.

By the time Thaddeus arrived in Washington, three other famous aeronauts had already offered their services. But Lowe had influential friends—Joseph Henry at the Smithsonian and Cincinnati newspaper editor Murat Halstead. They helped him gain favor with the government and arranged a meeting between Thaddeus and President Abraham Lincoln within days of Lowe's arrival in Washington.

At the meeting, Lowe described his plans for organizing a balloon corps. The president was looking for any new military technology that might shorten the conflict. He was particularly interested in Thaddeus's suggestion to direct artillery

# War Balloons

Ever since the launch of the first manned balloon, people recognized its military value. The French were the first to use observation balloons in battle during the 1790s. In this print, a French balloon floats above the 1794 Battle of Fleurus, Belgium, during which the French defeated the Austrians.

Several other European countries tried war balloons over the next fifty years. The U.S. Army considered using balloons during the Seminole War in Florida in the 1830s, but rejected the idea. In 1846, during the Mexican-American War, aeronaut John Wise suggested dropping bombs from a balloon. The army turned down his suggestion. The Civil War was the first time American war balloons took to the sky. These balloons were used for surveillance, not for air attacks.

**Joseph Henry (1797–1878)**
Henry was the most respected American scientist of his day and one of Thaddeus Lowe's strongest supporters. In 1846, Henry became the first director of the Smithsonian Institution in Washington. He encouraged scientific research in many fields and helped start a national weather service.

fire from a balloon when gunners couldn't see a faraway target. Lincoln encouraged Thaddeus to demonstrate what his balloon could do.

## TELEGRAM FOR THE PRESIDENT

To prove the balloon's value, Thaddeus had to show that he could give up-to-date information about the enemy from the air. How would he tell army officers on the ground what he was seeing from the balloon?

Lowe thought he had the solution—a telegraph wire that rapidly transmitted his message from the balloon to any place telegraph wires reached. No one had ever received a telegraphed signal sent from hundreds of feet above the ground. Thaddeus figured it was worth a try.

In mid-June, he prepared to launch the *Enterprise* in front of the Columbian Armory, not far from the Capitol building. As he inflated the balloon with city gas, the envelope dramatically rose from the ground.

Lowe climbed into the *Enterprise*'s basket with a telegraph operator and the superintendent of the American Telegraph Company. When Thaddeus gave the signal, his crew let out the ropes anchoring the balloon to the ground. Gradually, the *Enterprise* rose to about

# The Telegraph in the Civil War

The telegraph enabled military leaders to send messages to each other, often in secret code. Wherever the military needed telegraph lines, crews quickly strung wire on poles, trees, or fences. A battery wagon provided the electricity to operate the telegraph in the field.

Telegraph operators used Morse code to send messages, working in the heat of battle when necessary. Union and Confederate armies both tapped into and cut the telegraph lines of their opponent.

Thaddeus Lowe was the first to send telegraphed messages from a balloon.

**Uncoiling the Wire**
Photographer Timothy O'Sullivan shot this photograph of men hanging telegraph wire during the war.

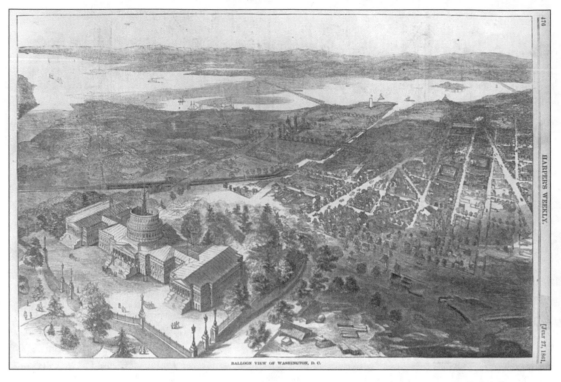

**Washington, 1861**
This engraving of Washington from the air appeared in *Harper's Weekly* on July 27, 1861. The Potomac River is in the background. The U.S. Capitol building, with its dome unfinished, is in the foreground. Thaddeus Lowe launched the *Enterprise* near the buildings at the center of the image, from a grassy area where the Smithsonian Institution's National Air and Space Museum stands today. His crew towed the balloon to the White House from this spot the same way character balloons are moved today in New York City's Thanksgiving Day Parade.

five hundred feet. The three men gazed out at Washington's streets and buildings, the unfinished Capitol dome, and thousands of soldiers' tents. They saw the fields and woods beyond the Potomac River, which was now the dividing line between North and South.

Lowe dictated his message to the telegraph operator in the balloon. "To President United States …" Using Morse code, the operator tapped out Lowe's words on a small telegraph unit. The signal traveled down a long wire to a station on the ground underneath the balloon. From there, it was transmitted to the War Department and the White House, where President Lincoln watched the balloon from the second floor. Another telegraph operator at that end wrote out Lowe's message.

The experiment worked! It was the first telegram ever sent from the sky.

From his years as an entertainer, Thaddeus knew how to hold an audience's attention. He called to his ground crew to lower the balloon and walk it several blocks to the White House—with the three men still standing in the basket.

An impressed President Lincoln invited Thaddeus to spend the night at the White House. The two men talked about a future balloon corps. Afterward, the president sent Lowe to discuss their plan with the head of the U.S. Army, General Winfield Scott. Lowe wrote later, "I was almost too excited to sleep, so enthused was I at the prospect of being directed to form a new branch of the military service."

Newspapers in both the North and South printed articles about Thaddeus and his balloon. One woman wrote to Lincoln from Philadelphia, suggesting how Lowe could help the Union cause: "Would it not be a grand idea to strike off hundreds of copies of your noble message [Lincoln's July 4 presidential message] and let Mr. Lowe ascend in his balloon and scatter them in Southern camps and all over the South— …"

*Continued on page 30*

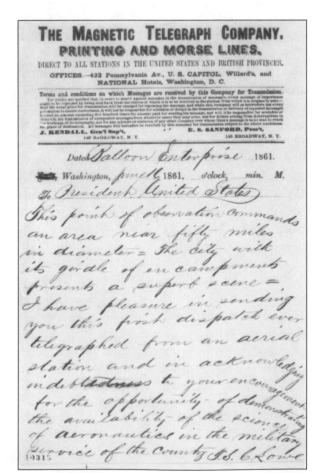

**Lowe's Telegram from the Air**
Thaddeus Lowe sent this telegram to President Abraham Lincoln from the *Enterprise*. Although the date appears to read June 16, Lowe's memoirs and press accounts at the time report that the telegram was sent on Tuesday, June 18. "This point of observation commands an area near fifty miles in diameter= The city with its girdle of encampments presents a superb scene= I have pleasure in sending you this first dispatch ever telegraphed from an aerial station and in acknowledging indebtedness to your encouragement for the opportunity of demonstrating the availability of the science of aeronautics in the military service of the country. T.S.C. Lowe"

**An Artist Sketches on the Battlefield**
Artist Alfred Waud sketched many of the Civil War images published in *Harper's Weekly*. Photographer Timothy O'Sullivan took this picture of Waud sketching the Gettysburg battlefield in early July 1863, a few days after the battle.

# Images of War

While the Civil War raged, photographers followed the armies, shooting thousands of pictures of battlefields and soldiers. Several photographers worked for Mathew Brady, who later collected many of the surviving Civil War images. Although Brady's name is often attached to these photographs, he did not take most of them. Many of the well-known images were by Alexander Gardner, Timothy O'Sullivan, James Gibson, and George Barnard.

It was difficult and dangerous to use the bulky photographic equipment in the middle of a battle. Instead, photographers usually took their battlefield photos after the fighting ended. They occasionally even added props, such as guns.

The public clamored to see images of the war. Photographs were displayed in galleries or sold as twenty-five-cent *cartes de visite*, picture cards about the size of today's trading cards. People also bought them on stereo view cards, in which two nearly identical photographs are printed side by side. When viewed through a handheld stereoscope, the image looks three-dimensional.

The technology to print photographs in newspapers did not yet exist. Publishers produced a drawing based on a photograph, then engraved the drawing into a wood block so that it could be printed.

Each week, *Harper's Weekly* and *Frank Leslie's Illustrated Newspaper* also published hand-drawn illustrations of the war. Artists traveled with the troops and sketched war scenes. They sent their drawings from the battlefront to the publishers, who engraved the drawings into wood blocks for printing.

Thaddeus Lowe took artists up in his balloon so that they could sketch the view from the sky. Historians do not know of any aerial photographs shot from a balloon during the Civil War, although photographers tried at least once. In Virginia, in July 1862, one of Lowe's assistant aeronauts, James Allen, took up some photographers. But a strong wind prevented them from shooting any good photos.

### General Winfield Scott (1786–1866)

At the beginning of the Civil War, Scott was the general in chief of the U.S. Army. He had served in the army for more than fifty years, including twenty years as its commander. Admired for his military abilities, Scott was popular enough to run for president in 1852, although he lost. Thaddeus Lowe considered Scott to be too old and set in his ways to appreciate the value of a balloon corps. After the Union loss at the Battle of Bull Run, political pressure from senators led to Scott's retirement in the fall of 1861.

### Mathew Brady (1823?–96)

At the time of the Civil War, Mathew Brady was a well-known American photographer, noted for his portraits of famous people. Partly because of his efforts, thousands of images document the war.

**Abraham Lincoln (1809–65) with His Eleven-Year-Old Son Tad**
Although Lincoln never went up in Lowe's balloon, he encouraged the use of spy balloons and other new military inventions. He is the only U.S. president to hold a patent, receiving one in 1849 for a device that lifts a boat from a sandbar. Alexander Gardner took this photograph in his Washington studio on Sunday, February 5, 1865. A few weeks later, on April 14, Lincoln was assassinated.

## THADDEUS THE SPY

A few days after his meeting with President Lincoln, Thaddeus received a message from the U.S. Army Corps of Topographical Engineers at the Washington hotel where he was staying. The corps was in charge of drawing maps that officers used when they moved troops and planned battles. The army had few accurate maps of the South. A balloon view of the Virginia landscape could help mapmakers see important features such as roads, hills, streams, and woods.

At the army's direction, Lowe inflated the *Enterprise* with city gas. A crew of twenty soldiers towed the balloon several miles to an army position on the outskirts of Washington. Over the next few days, Thaddeus took up army officers so that they could check the location of Rebel forces.

One soldier went up to draw a map. His superior officer reported that "the map of the country, rough as it is, which he made during the ascent, convince me that a balloon may at times greatly assist military movements."

The Confederates immediately spotted Lowe overhead. But a Rebel soldier camped outside of Washington was apparently unconcerned about the balloon spy.

In early July, he reported, "The Baloon experiment was an utter failure—This place could not be seen from the Balloon, and it was taken back to Washington, where Professor Lowe and the Rail Splitter [President Lincoln] performed some interesting and highly scientific feats."

Richmond's *Daily Dispatch*, a newspaper published in the Confederate capital, carried a story about Thaddeus. "Prof. Lowe brought his balloon, inflated, from Arlington Heights this morning ... intending to make an ascension ... but the wind was too high."

Even though the weather sometimes prevented Lowe from going up, his successful flights made Confederate commanders uneasy. General P. G. T. Beauregard worried that "the infernal balloon" would give away Rebel troop strength and camp locations. He ordered tents to be set up in the woods so that they couldn't be counted. He wanted nighttime lights either covered or not used at all, and cannons hidden with leaves and brush.

With his competitors still vying to be the leader of an army balloons corps, Lowe worked even harder to win the position. He considered himself the only man with the necessary knowledge and skills. He wrote later, "Neither [John Wise nor John La Mountain] had the least idea of the requirements of military ballooning nor the gift of invention which later made it possible for me to achieve success."

Throughout July, Thaddeus continued to promote himself by taking up army officials and reporters in his tethered balloon on the Smithsonian Institution grounds. Joseph Henry helped by making an official report to the secretary of war, praising Lowe's work.

## SUNDAY BATTLE IN MANASSAS

The public pressure had mounted on President Lincoln and the Northern generals to strike the Confederate troops gathered in Manassas, Virginia. Finally, Union soldiers marched from Washington and attacked on July 21, 1861. Many people followed in horses and carriages to watch the Sunday battle, the Battle of Bull Run, as Northerners called it. They expected an easy victory to end the Southern rebellion. Instead, the Union army fell apart in defeat.

The Confederate victory at Manassas shocked the North. Rumors spread through

Washington that the Rebels were about to cross the Potomac River and attack the city. Thaddeus Lowe saw a chance to use his balloon to find out if this was true.

A few days after the battle, Lowe made a free flight in the *Enterprise* over the area between Manassas and the Union lines outside of Washington. Flying high above Confederate territory, he saw no Rebel troops moving toward the city.

Relieved, Thaddeus was eager to return to the capital and share the news. He caught an eastward air current. But as he started to land near Washington, he heard shots and whistling bullets from Union guns below.

"Show [your] colors," the Northern soldiers shouted up to him.

They thought he was the enemy! Thaddeus had no flag in his basket to prove he

**Forts Around Washington**
To protect the capital, the Union army built more than sixty forts around the city. The Confederates never entered Washington's city limits during the war. These Union soldiers man a cannon at Fort Corcoran in Arlington, Virginia, near the headquarters of the Balloon Corps during fall and winter 1861–62.

was on their side. To steer clear of their guns, he had to sail away and bring down the balloon in some trees—two miles beyond the Union lines.

Before Confederate soldiers could find him, Lowe quickly released the gas from the balloon and gathered up the envelope, which had been damaged in the landing. Then he hid. Fortunately, Union soldiers stationed on the front lines had seen the balloon go down, and they came to his rescue.

Lowe's observations from the air reassured people in Washington that the Rebel army was not ready to attack. But his close call convinced Thaddeus that free-flight spying was too dangerous. An aeronaut might be captured and his balloon used by the Confederates against the Union. Lowe later criticized one of his competitors, John La Mountain, for taking such risks.

## CONVINCING A GENERAL

By the end of July, more than a month had passed since President Lincoln first encouraged Lowe. Thaddeus had been using his own balloon equipment and receiving no pay for the observations he made. Yet General Winfield Scott still had not set up a balloon corps or made Lowe its head. Every time Thaddeus tried to visit the seventy-five-year-old general at army headquarters, Scott made excuses to avoid seeing him. Finally, Lowe returned to the White House to report his problem to President Lincoln.

*Continued on page 36*

**Lincoln's Note**
Four days after the Union defeat at the Battle of Bull Run, President Lincoln wrote this note to General Winfield Scott, who had failed to discuss the balloon corps with Lowe. After receiving the note, Scott still refused to meet with the balloonist—until Lincoln showed up in the general's office with Lowe.

## Lowe's Competitors

### James Allen (1824–97)

Allen (left) was a well-known aeronaut in New England. At the start of the war, he volunteered as a balloonist with a regiment from his home state of Rhode Island. Allen arrived in Washington in early June 1861 with two balloons, but he didn't stay long. One balloon burst when it was inflated. The other struck a telegraph pole in a high wind and ripped.

The military considered Allen's balloons a failure, and he returned to Rhode Island. Thaddeus Lowe, however, recognized Allen's ballooning skills and experience. Several months later, in February 1862, he asked James Allen to join the Balloon Corps.

### John Wise (1808–79)

In June 1861, the U.S. government asked Wise to build and fly a war balloon. His first assignment came in late July when the Union and Confederate armies faced each other at the Battle of Bull Run, not far from Washington. As soldiers guided Wise's inflated balloon from Washington to the battlefield, it was torn by tree branches. Wise missed the battle.

A few days later, the wind carried off the mended balloon while a crew was moving it. Afraid that the Confederates might capture the balloon, Union soldiers shot it down. By August, Wise and the army had given up on each other, and Wise went home to Pennsylvania.

**La Mountain in the Air**
This illustration from *Frank Leslie's Illustrated Newspaper* shows John La Mountain making observations near Fort Monroe in August 1861.

## John La Mountain (1830?–70)

John La Mountain's daring balloon voyages made headlines for two years before the Civil War began. In June 1861, the Union general at Fort Monroe asked La Mountain for his help. The fort was strategically located at the tip of the Virginia peninsula, and the Union did not want to lose control of it to the Confederates. The aeronaut headed south with two balloons from his home in Troy, New York. He kept an eye on the Rebels surrounding the fort while the balloon was tethered either to the ground or a boat.

After a new general took command of Fort Monroe in September, La Mountain was sent to Washington and hired as a balloonist with the Army of the Potomac. Unlike Lowe, who stayed anchored to the ground and often took up army officers with him, La Mountain made free flights alone. He launched into a westward wind that carried him over Confederate lines, high enough to be out of gun range. When he finished his observations, he returned to Union territory by taking his balloon into the eastward air current. Since he had no contact with the ground the way Lowe did, La Mountain couldn't give his report until he landed. He brought back useful information, but his free-flight method was risky. Winds could be unpredictable. During one landing, La Mountain was shot at by Union soldiers who thought he was a Confederate spy.

Perhaps because of jealousy, Lowe and La Mountain disliked each other and were unable to cooperate. But Lowe had the support of the commanding generals. The aeronauts' disagreements led to La Mountain's dismissal by the army in February 1862. He returned to civilian life and died in 1870 from natural causes.

The president was irritated when he heard that General Scott had repeatedly ignored Thaddeus. Lincoln believed that information from a balloon might have changed the disastrous outcome of the Bull Run battle. He grabbed his hat and told Thaddeus to follow him. The two strode a couple of blocks to army headquarters.

The president made his intentions clear to Scott. "General, this is my friend Professor Lowe, who is organizing an Aeronautic Corps for the Army, and is to be its Chief." He went on, "I wish you … to give him all the necessary things to equip his branch of the service on land and water."

Thanks to President Lincoln, Lowe got what he wanted. On August 2, the Topographical Engineers hired him to construct and operate a new war balloon at a cost of $1,500. Without delay, Lowe headed back to his Philadelphia factory to build the *Union*.

CHAPTER FOUR

# The Balloon Corps Is Born

One month later, at the end of August 1861, Thaddeus Lowe returned to Washington with the new spy balloon, the *Union*.

President Abraham Lincoln had just appointed General George McClellan as commander of the Army of the Potomac. Lincoln hoped that McClellan could prevent another humiliating Union defeat like the one at the Battle of Bull Run. McClellan was responsible for guarding the capital and training the soldiers in Washington.

Confederate troops were within five miles of the city. The Union army wanted to know what its enemy was doing, and Lowe's spy balloon could supply that information. The Topographical Engineers immediately gave Thaddeus an assignment at their fort near Arlington, Virginia, across the Potomac River from Washington.

At the aeronaut's request, the army provided thirty soldiers as a balloon crew. With their help, Thaddeus inflated the *Union* at the Columbian Armory and towed it across the bridge to Arlington. On August 29, he went up in the balloon and spotted the Rebels building new fortifications on nearby hills.

During the next few weeks, army officers ordered him to take up the balloon almost every day and often at night. At times, a commander needed information about an area that Lowe couldn't see from above his base near Fort Corcoran. The aeronaut and his crew then towed the *Union* to a better launch site.

Whenever Lowe ascended, he made sure that three or four cables anchored the balloon. His crew held the cables or used pulleys attached to trees. Thaddeus trained the men to control the cables, carefully letting them out or hauling them in on his

## George B. McClellan (1826–85)

Like many Civil War commanders on both sides, General George B. McClellan was educated at the U.S. Military Academy at West Point and fought in the Mexican-American War. Beginning in the late summer of 1861, he organized and headed the Army of the Potomac, a division of the Union army.

After General Scott retired in November 1861, Lincoln appointed McClellan as general in chief of the entire Union army. Although McClellan was popular with the soldiers, President Lincoln did not think he was aggressive enough in fighting the Confederates. In March 1862, Lincoln removed him as general in chief, allowing McClellan to keep command of the Army of the Potomac. But in November 1862, Lincoln gave up on McClellan, stripping him of his command.

McClellan ran against Lincoln as the Democratic nominee in the 1864 presidential election and lost. In his later years, he worked in business and became governor of New Jersey. In this wartime photograph, McClellan poses with his wife, Mary Ellen. Historians have learned about the general's thoughts and emotions during the war from the daily letters he wrote her.

instructions from the basket. Some of the ropes were nearly a mile (5,280 feet) long, although Lowe usually went up only 500 to 1,000 feet. Using his spyglass from that height, he could see for many miles.

When the *Union* needed more gas, Thaddeus and the crew towed it back to Washington for reinflation from the city gas supply. Lowe sometimes made the trip in the basket, directing the men as they managed the ropes. The crew never snagged the balloon in telegraph poles or trees as other aeronauts had.

Lowe's only serious accident occurred during a severe windstorm in October 1861. To hold down the *Union*, Thaddeus and his men lashed the cables to tree stumps. But the blowing wind whipped at the balloon, straining the cords of the mesh net surrounding the envelope. Finally, the cords broke. The silk envelope soared away, leaving behind the basket and broken ropes. The wind carried the *Union* a hundred miles before it came down in Delaware.

Four men found the balloon and hid it. Suspected of supporting the Rebels, the men were soon arrested for concealing a government balloon "with treasonable purpose." After being held as prisoners of war for two weeks, the men took an oath of allegiance to the United

States. The balloon was returned to Lowe. He repaired the envelope and put the *Union* back into service. Once again, he had seen the power of wind.

## WATCHING THE REBELS

As Lowe took up more army officers and made more observations, he learned to interpret what he saw. He estimated soldier numbers by counting tents and campfires. He was able to distinguish between smoke from burning trash or cooking fires and smoke created by rifles or cannons. When Thaddeus saw dust clouds on the roads, he knew that troops were moving. He could even tell whether the dust was made by marching soldiers, by cavalry horses, or by horses and wagons.

In one September dispatch to a commander about Confederate positions outside of Washington, Lowe wrote, "During my observations this evening I noticed a pretty heavy picket force on Upton's Hill and several camp smokes at Taylor's Corners. On the west slope of Munson's Hill there appeared to be a full regiment with a set of colors, their bayonets glistening in the sun as if on parade."

The Confederates watched the balloon anxiously. General James Longstreet, on whose brigade Lowe was spying, later wrote that the Rebels felt secure until "the Federals [the Union army] began to realize all of their advantages by floating balloons above our heads."

As a result, the *Union* became a frequent target. One Rebel officer, Edward Porter Alexander, wrote his father, "We sent a rifle shell so near old Lowe and his balloon that he came down as fast as gravity could bring him."

It took nerve to go up in the balloon when the Confederates were aiming at it. Thaddeus knew he couldn't stop the Rebel shots. But he tried to reduce the chance that the balloon or its passengers might be hit. Whenever possible, he launched from behind a hill or stand of trees, out of the Rebels' view. Sometimes he directed his crew to cut evergreen trees and anchor them in the ground around the launch site. The thick boughs hid the balloon and shielded it from wind.

As soon as the balloon rose above the trees, the Confederate artillery guns and rifles often opened fire. But once the spy balloon floated above five hundred feet, it was out of shooting range. The aeronaut and his passengers were safe—until the balloon came down.

## AIMING THE ARTILLERY

On September 24, 1861, Lowe got his first chance to test the use of balloons in aiming artillery. One of the Union generals planned to fire artillery at a target in Falls Church, Virginia, which the gunners couldn't see. The general requested a report from the balloon. "During the time of fire," he ordered, "it is very important to know how much the shot or shell fall short, if any at all."

He asked Lowe to send his observations by both telegraph and flag signals. "If we fire to the right of Falls Church," he instructed, "let a white flag be raised in the balloon; if to the left, let it be lowered; if over, let it be shown stationary; if under, let it be waved occasionally."

Thaddeus took the *Union* up to one thousand feet at Fort Corcoran, about three miles from the gunners. As the artillery guns fired, he looked for signs of impact and explosion in the distance. Then he signaled with his flag from the balloon. Observers with the gunners watched Lowe's signals through field glasses, passing on the information so that the gunners could adjust their aim. It was the first time in history that artillery fire was aimed from the sky.

**Lowe's Equipment**
Lowe's gas generators sit on a grassy area in Washington in late 1861 or early 1862. Today this spot is on the Washington Mall directly in front of the Smithsonian Institution's National Air and Space Museum. The generators were painted pale blue. The black lettering on the back of the left one says "Lowe's Balloon Gas Generator."
In the background is the unfinished dome of the Capitol, which was completed by the end of the war.

**Lowe and Father**
Thaddeus Lowe and his father, Clovis, are photographed in front of their tent during the war. Clovis Lowe (left), who was in his sixties, served eighteen months as his son's assistant in charge of repairing and operating the balloon equipment. Thaddeus and at least three of his brothers served with the Union army.

## FRIENDS IN HIGH PLACES

Unlike the disinterested and elderly General Scott, General George McClellan was enthusiastic about the spy balloons. Just six years older than Lowe, the young general had a background in engineering and had studied new military techniques in Europe. In early September, the *New York Times* noted his first balloon trip: "Gen. McClellan on Saturday made a balloon assention with Prof. Lowe, and spent two hours in making reconnoisances of the enemy's positions."

McClellan realized how balloons might be used against the enemy. He arranged for Thaddeus to report directly to his aide, General Fitz John Porter, who had already been up with Lowe.

After Lowe had been making observations from the *Union* for only two weeks, Porter told him, "You are of value now." He asked Lowe what he needed to form a balloon corps that could move with the army and operate at several locations at the same time.

This is what Thaddeus had hoped for. He proposed two more balloons and the portable gas machines to inflate them when city gas was unavailable. Instead,

## Lowe's Portable Gas Generator

Thaddeus Lowe designed the first mobile hydrogen gas generator used in war. The generator's copper-lined wooden tank—eleven feet long and five feet high—fit on the frame of an army wagon. A team of four horses pulled it from place to place. The army eventually ordered twelve generators, which were built for about five hundred dollars each at the Washington Navy Yard.

The balloon crew made hydrogen gas by adding iron filings, sulfuric acid, and water through openings in the top of the tank. When the iron and acid mixed inside the tank, a chemical reaction produced a hot gas.

The gas flowed from the tank through a rubber hose to a wooden box filled with water. There it cooled. Next, the gas flowed to the purifier box. This box was filled with lime and water to absorb extra gases produced in the process. (See the two small boxes on the right of the photograph.) The purified hydrogen then flowed into the balloon, which was attached to the box on the right of the photograph. One generator produced enough hydrogen to fill a balloon in three hours.

General McClellan asked the secretary of war to authorize *four* balloons with gas generators. Thaddeus would be paid $1,500 for each large balloon and $1,200 for each smaller one.

Pleased with the news, Lowe directed his Philadelphia factory to start work right away. He designed the new war balloons to be sturdier than regular balloons. The silk envelopes were coated with extra layers of varnish. This made the balloons strong enough to withstand wind and wet weather and able to hold gas for more than two weeks without refilling. After powerful winds broke the *Union*'s netting, Lowe added extra-sturdy cords to the new balloons.

In late September, the Army of the Potomac officially hired Thaddeus as "Chief Aeronaut to the Army of the United States." He had accomplished his goal. Immediately, Thaddeus began hiring a team of aeronauts and assistants, most of whom had experience in ballooning. He supervised the other aeronauts and all balloon operations. Lowe was paid ten dollars a day, which was close to what an army colonel earned. His assistant aeronauts received about half that amount.

The army classified Lowe and the Balloon Corps as civilian employees.

# The Balloon Corps

Chief Aeronaut Thaddeus Lowe hired about a dozen men as aeronauts and assistants, many of whom he had known before the war began. Historians have collected information about only a few of them.

**William Paullin** was the first aeronaut hired by Lowe in October 1861. He had almost thirty years of experience flying balloons and had worked with Lowe before. Paullin was stationed on the lower Potomac River at Budd's Ferry, Maryland, until January 1862. When his side business as a photographer interfered with his aeronaut duties, Lowe dismissed him.

**John Starkweather**, an aeronaut from Boston, joined the Balloon Corps in November 1861. On General McClellan's orders, Lowe sent him with a balloon to South Carolina. Starkweather returned home the next June after the balloon was damaged by winds.

**Ebenezer Seaver (left) and John Starkweather**
The two gave this photograph to Thaddeus Lowe, probably during the winter of 1861–62.

**Ebenezer Seaver** was hired in mid-November 1861 as an assistant aeronaut. **Ebenezer Mason**, from Troy, New York, joined in December 1861 and oversaw balloon construction in Lowe's Philadelphia factory. Both Seaver and Mason worked at balloon bases along the Potomac and around Washington. They went with the Balloon Corps to the Virginia peninsula in spring 1862. But within weeks, the two refused to work because the government had not paid their salaries. Lowe fired them.

**John Steiner**, a German immigrant, was a well-known balloonist before Lowe hired him in December 1861. For a while, Steiner was stationed on the upper Potomac River, where commanders made frequent use of his balloon. His time along the Mississippi River, from February to June 1862, was less productive. By the end of 1862, Steiner had left the Balloon Corps because he had not been paid.

**Jacob Freno** helped Lowe launch his April 1861 flight from Cincinnati, Ohio, to South Carolina. Lowe hired him in January 1862 to take over Steiner's position on the upper Potomac River. He fired Freno less than a year later for gambling and taking leaves without permission.

**James Allen**, an experienced Rhode Island aeronaut, joined the Balloon Corps in March 1862. His brother **Ezra Allen** joined in fall 1862. James temporarily took over Lowe's duties in the summer of 1862 while Lowe recovered from a severe fever. The Allen brothers operated the balloons after Lowe resigned in May 1863 until the Balloon Corps disbanded that summer.

**The First Aircraft Carrier**
An unknown artist made this drawing of the balloon boat *George Washington Parke Custis* in November 1861 when Thaddeus Lowe and John Starkweather visited Budd's Ferry with the balloon *Washington*. The gas generators sit on the far end of the boat's deck. The acid and iron filings used to produce hydrogen gas are stored at the opposite end. Custis (1781–1857) was George Washington's stepgrandson and the father-in-law of Confederate general Robert E. Lee.

Thaddeus argued that the corps should be a branch of the army and that he should be made a military officer. He was worried that the aeronauts might be hanged as spies if they were captured, because they did not wear army uniforms. Despite Lowe's arguments, the Balloon Corps remained a civilian group working for the army.

## THE FIRST AIRCRAFT CARRIER

By early November 1861, the four new balloons were finished—the *Intrepid, Constitution, United States,* and *Washington.* "I have now a competent aeronaut for each of the new balloons," Lowe reported to General McClellan's headquarters, "and in the course of a few days they can all be in active operation."

McClellan had just been promoted to general in chief of the entire Union army after General Scott retired. He had plans for the Balloon Corps. Confederate troops held positions on the Virginia side of the Potomac River northwest and south of Washington. Union officers needed information. How many enemy troops were in these areas? Had they established new camps? Were large groups of soldiers traveling along the roads?

# The Balloons

Lowe's factory in Philadelphia built seven balloons for the army between August 1861 and January 1862. The larger balloons lifted more passengers. The smaller ones inflated faster, were easier to move, and better withstood winds and extreme weather. If the weather was calm, all balloons could be fully inflated and had double the normal lifting power.

The envelopes were decorated with paintings of the bald eagle, the United States flag, or famous Americans such as George Washington. The wicker baskets were painted blue with white stars, and some included red and white stripes. Besides looking artistic, the designs told Union troops that the balloons were friendly.

The *Union* and *Intrepid* could lift five men under normal conditions. Their envelopes were about as tall as a five-story building and held 32,000 cubic feet of gas.

The *Constitution* and *United States* held 25,000 cubic feet of gas and could lift three men.

The *Washington* held 20,000 cubic feet of gas and lifted two men.

The *Eagle* and *Excelsior* held 15,000 cubic feet of gas and usually carried one man. The envelopes of these smaller balloons were about the height of a three-story building.

**The *Intrepid* Takes to the Air**

This engraving of an artist's sketch appeared in *Harper's Weekly*, December 14, 1861. It shows Lowe about to ascend in the *Intrepid* to observe Confederate positions outside Washington.

General McClellan ordered the Balloon Corps to join several separate divisions of the Army of the Potomac on the north side of the river. The aeronauts were to watch for surprise attacks and to take up officers for observations.

Lowe suggested that the aeronauts could see more enemy positions if they ascended from a boat in the river. The secretary of the navy allowed Lowe to turn a barge into a balloon boat, complete with gas generator. A steam-powered tugboat towed the barge, called the *George Washington Parke Custis*, with a balloon anchored on the deck. It was the first military aircraft carrier.

On November 10, the Balloon Corps used the boat for the first time. Thaddeus and assistant aeronaut William Paullin took the *Constitution* downriver from Washington to General Joseph Hooker's command near Budd's Ferry, Maryland. The Confederates across the Potomac River had been firing cannons at boats, trying to cut off traffic from the Chesapeake Bay to Washington.

Once the balloon boat was in place, Lowe and Paullin inflated the *Constitution* using the new gas generator. Then they ascended from the balloon boat with a Union officer to check the Confederate forces. Lowe reported back to army headquarters in Washington, "We had a fine view of the enemy's camp-fires during the evening, and saw the rebels constructing new batteries. …"

The Confederates wasted little time firing on the *Constitution*. A young Union soldier near Budd's Ferry wrote to his parents in New Hampshire, "As soon as it became inflated so the rebels could see it they commenced throwing shells at it … The shell passed directly over our heads … and exploded the instant it struck the ground."

In addition to the balloons at Budd's Ferry and Washington, General McClellan ordered one sent to Edwards Ferry, Maryland, on the upper Potomac River. Union commanders used the balloon to spy on the Confederates across the river near Leesburg, Virginia. More than once, Rebel sharpshooters aimed at the balloon. One day, a soldier riding in the *Intrepid* with aeronaut John Steiner had his hat shot off.

## BALLOONS SOUTH AND WEST

General McClellan also stationed a balloon along the coast of South Carolina. The Union was trying to maintain a blockade of the Southern harbors along the Atlantic coast, in order to prevent supplies from getting through to the

# Mapmaking

Starting in late June 1861, Union army mapmakers ascended in balloons to draw the landscape and mark enemy positions. Sometimes army officers asked the aeronauts to add detail to existing maps, including fortifications and camps.

In late fall 1861, General George McClellan ordered an aerial map drawn of the Rebel positions on the lower Potomac River. Colonel William Small produced this map from the air near Budd's Ferry, Maryland.

Aeronaut William Paullin took Small up in the *Constitution* to seven hundred feet several times during December 8 and 9, 1861. While Rebel gunners shot unsuccessfully at the balloon, Small sketched Confederate gun batteries and nine camps on the Virginia side of the Potomac River. (See the top half of the map.) He added the balloon to show that the map was based on an aerial observation. Small later reported, "Mr. Paullin, the aeronaut in charge of the balloon, is entitled to much credit for the skill and zeal displayed in conducting the ascensions. ..."

**Small's Map at Budd's Ferry**

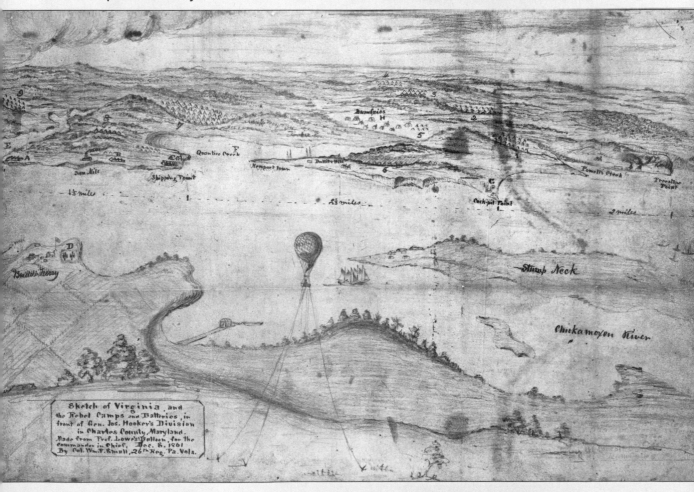

## "Masterly Inactivity, or Six Months on the Potomac"

This political cartoon, which poked fun at the Yankee and Rebel armies' standoff across the Potomac River, appeared in *Frank Leslie's Illustrated Newspaper* on February 1, 1862.

Confederates. Lowe sent aeronaut John Starkweather with the *Washington* and two gas generators.

When Starkweather arrived in early January 1862, he was not welcomed. The general in charge had not asked for a spy balloon and had no plans to use it. For three months, the aeronaut never left the ground.

Finally in April, a new army commander took over. He asked Starkweather to get to work taking up officers in the *Washington*. From the balloon, they discovered Rebel camps, monitored the building of a Confederate ironclad gunboat, and spied on defenses of nearby Savannah, Georgia.

Starkweather's problems weren't over, though. He had trouble receiving shipments of acid and iron to make hydrogen gas. Ocean winds made it difficult to use the balloon. In June 1862, a strong wind ripped the *Washington*, and Starkweather didn't have the materials to fix it. With no other choice, he boarded a boat north to New York with the damaged balloon. Balloon Corps operations in South Carolina were over.

Besides the balloons in South Carolina and along the Potomac River, General McClellan assigned one to Union forces fighting for control of the Mississippi River. The river gave the Union an invasion path into the South. Lowe sent aeronaut John Steiner west with the *Eagle*, one of the two smaller balloons built in December. By late February 1862, Steiner arrived in Cairo, Illinois, at the state's southern tip.

Just as Starkweather had found in South Carolina, the army commanders along the Mississippi weren't interested in the spy balloon. Steiner used the balloon for only a single week during his five-month assignment.

In March, he volunteered to help the Union navy attack a Confederate fortification on Island No. 10 in the Mississippi River. Operating the *Eagle* from a boat, Steiner took up officers who directed the aim of Union mortars against Confederate artillery guns. The Rebels eventually surrendered their position on the island.

Aeronaut Steiner was frustrated that the generals didn't use the balloon more often. He wrote Lowe in early June 1862, using poor spelling: "I am satisfyde that Gen. Halleck [the Union commander] is no friend to the Aeronautick Core. I could have bin of grade servis at Corince [Corinth, Mississippi]."

**Quaker Guns**
After the Confederate army withdrew from northern Virginia in spring 1862, Union troops discovered logs made to look like cannons. Called Quaker guns, these dummy guns fooled commanders into thinking the Rebels had more weapons than they did. This photograph of Union soldiers standing by abandoned Confederate Quaker guns was taken in Centreville, Virginia, in March 1862.

Steiner was right. In late May 1862, the Confederate commander at Corinth was General Beauregard, who had earlier hidden his camps from balloons along the Potomac. To fool Union forces into thinking the Confederates were about to attack, Beauregard used Quaker guns (fake cannons) and misleading campfires. Meanwhile, he secretly moved his outnumbered troops away from Corinth. All the time, the Confederate commander worried that Steiner's Union balloon might uncover his deception. When Beauregard heard that there was no Union balloon in the area, despite the rumors, he wrote to another general, "I am glad to hear of the sham balloon. I hope it is so, for I fear that more than their artillery at this moment."

## LEAVING THE POTOMAC RIVER

Throughout the fall and winter of 1861–62, the two armies eyed each other warily across the Potomac River. Thaddeus Lowe supervised the balloon stations along the river, using the balloon boat to move equipment and supplies from base to base. He passed along orders from army headquarters and conveyed the aeronauts' reports to commanders. Thaddeus also continued making balloon observations himself.

Then during the first days of March 1862, Lowe noticed something different along the Confederate lines in northern Virginia. From the balloon, he reported that there were "more smokes than usual. ..." The Rebels were abandoning their camps and burning what they couldn't take with them.

For more than six months, the Confederates sat just outside Washington. The Union commanders never realized that their enemy lacked the strength to attack the capital. Now the Rebels had sneaked away and headed south.

CHAPTER FIVE

# "The Most Shot-At Man in the War"

President Lincoln was frustrated when General McClellan did not attack the Confederate army during the months it was gathered near Washington. The two men did not get along well personally or agree on strategy. In early March 1862, Lincoln removed McClellan as general in chief of all United States forces, leaving him with command of the Army of the Potomac.

After the Rebel army moved south, McClellan developed a plan to attack the Confederate capital of Richmond, Virginia. The Army of the Potomac would approach the city from the east along the Virginia peninsula, the land lying between the York and James rivers.

By mid-March, McClellan had begun transferring his army from Washington to Fort Monroe on the tip of the peninsula. The Balloon Corps went, too, joining more than 120,000 men and thousands of horses, wagons, guns, and supplies.

They traveled in boats down the Potomac River, into the Chesapeake Bay, and on to the fort. The soldiers' battle cry was "On to Richmond."

As soon as Thaddeus Lowe arrived at Fort Monroe, he received orders from General McClellan. The first balloon was to go with General Fitz John Porter's

**General Fitz John Porter (1822–1901)**
Porter was one of the Balloon Corps' strongest supporters. A graduate of West Point, he was a division commander in the Army of the Potomac and General George McClellan's close adviser.

**Balloon Over the York River**
In spring 1862, artist Arthur Lumley went up in Lowe's balloon and made this sketch of the Confederate forts and camps at Yorktown, Virginia. He added the balloon to show that the drawing was a balloon view. From a height of a thousand feet, Lowe and Lumley saw thirty miles up and down the river. The engraving appeared in *Frank Leslie's Illustrated Newspaper*.

advance force on its march up the peninsula. Richmond was about seventy miles from the fort, and General McClellan wanted to know where the Confederates had set up their defenses. The balloons could get him that information.

The army assigned fifty soldiers from nearby regiments to each of the balloon crews. The men manned the ropes during launches, made repairs to the balloons, operated the gas generators, and delivered messages. They also set up the balloon camps. Lowe chose sites near a stream or pond where he could get enough water to run the generators.

By the evening of April 5, Lowe had used two gas generators to inflate the *Intrepid* near Yorktown, about twenty miles from Fort Monroe. He and an army officer went aloft to check out the locations of Rebel troops and wagons. While the balloon swayed in the breeze, Thaddeus had his first look at the panorama of woods and fields lying between the York and James rivers. He gazed down at men poised to battle each other. Staring up at him, hundreds of soldiers had *their* first glimpse of the silk balloon that "glistened … like a ball of silver suspended in the air."

At dawn the next day, Lowe and General Porter ascended a thousand feet into the clear sky for nearly two hours. Less than a mile away were Confederate earthworks, tents, and artillery. Thaddeus and the general realized that the Rebel defenses were strong. Later that day, Thaddeus took up draftsmen to sketch maps of the enemy positions.

General McClellan was pleased with the information. "The balloon has been of great service to-day," he wrote.

Meanwhile, the Confederate commander at Yorktown notified his superior officers in Richmond, "Balloons have been observing Yorktown and the whole of our line. They discovered a weak point … We will work day and night to strength it."

## DANGER FOR A GENERAL

Thaddeus was ordered to prepare a second balloon, the *Constitution*, for observations several miles away. He left assistant aeronaut James Allen in charge of the *Intrepid* at General Porter's camp. All did not go well while Lowe was gone.

**Lowe Supervises Inflation**
During the Peninsula Campaign in spring 1862, Lowe stands to the right of the *Intrepid* with his hand on the envelope, testing for the correct amount of gas. Because Lowe had no access to city gas, his hydrogen generators were the only way to inflate Union balloons. This photograph was probably taken by James Gibson either on May 31 or June 1, 1862.

**Porter Monument**
An engraving on a monument in honor of General Fitz John Porter, at his birthplace of Portsmouth, New Hampshire, shows him spying on Confederate camps from a balloon basket. Porter's spectacular accidental free flight in April 1862 was witnessed by thousands of soldiers on both sides. Many of them wrote about it in their letters home or in their memoirs years later.

At first light on the morning of April 11, 1862, Porter told Allen to ready the *Intrepid* for an ascension. The general had been in the balloons many times since the previous summer, and he intended to go up alone to inspect the Rebel defenses. Porter climbed into the basket, and the crew let out the single anchor rope. The balloon gradually rose several hundred feet into the dawn sky.

Suddenly, the rope snapped. The *Intrepid* broke loose and lifted up and away.

"O-pen-the-valve! … The valve!" shouted voices on the ground.

But before Porter could pull the valve cord, the wind blew the yellow-tinged balloon over Confederate lines. Thousands of Union soldiers watching in nearby camps held their breath. Would the enemy capture one of the Union's top generals *and* its largest war balloon in use?

While the *Intrepid* drifted back and forth from Rebel to Yankee territory during the next hour, General Porter studied the enemy's defenses through his long, black spyglass. A few Rebel soldiers shot their muskets at the balloon, but it was too high to hit.

Finally the wind brought the balloon back over the Union camps again. The general coolly stretched above the basket to reach the valve cord. As he pulled, the hydrogen gas whooshed through the open valve at the top of the balloon. The deflated envelope formed a silk parachute, breaking Porter's plunge to the ground. He was greeted with cheers, as more than a dozen Union soldiers grabbed the basket.

Lowe returned on horseback as Porter landed, and he was angry. Against his rules, James Allen had tethered the balloon with only one rope.

## George Armstrong Custer (1839–76)

Custer (right) is best known for "Custer's Last Stand," when he led a doomed 1876 cavalry attack against Lakota and Cheyenne Indians in the Battle of the Little Bighorn, Montana.

During the Peninsula Campaign in April 1862, Lieutenant Custer was ordered to make observations and draw maps from a balloon. Although he was known for his nerve and daring, he later admitted his fear during his first flight with aeronaut James Allen. "I remained seated in the bottom of the basket with a firm hold upon either side." When Allen jumped up and down to prove that the wicker basket was safe, Custer expected "one or both of us [to be] dashed to the earth." Eventually, Custer grew to enjoy the "magnificent scenery" and appreciate the value of the spy balloon.

In this photograph by James Gibson, Custer poses with his West Point classmate James B. Washington, a Confederate officer captured in late May 1862 at the Battle of Fair Oaks. The child is Washington's slave, who accompanied him to war.

Spilled acid used in the gas generators had eaten through the rope, causing it to break as the balloon rose. Thaddeus had worked hard to convince army commanders that balloons were a safe and effective way to spy on the enemy. Later he complained, "I found it difficult for a time to restore confidence among the officers. ..."

General McClellan was one who lost confidence. He wrote his wife about Porter's near-disastrous ride. "I am just recovering from a terrible scare," he told her. "You may rest assured of one thing: you won't catch me in the confounded balloon nor will I allow any other Generals to go up in it!"

Fortunately for the Balloon Corps, McClellan soon forgot his vow. Within a couple of days, the general once again ordered Lowe to take up officers to spy on the enemy.

## SIEGE AT YORKTOWN

To block the Union's advance to Richmond, the Confederate army set up its defenses from Yorktown on the York River across the peninsula to the James River. General McClellan thought that the Rebels had many more troops defending this line than they actually did. He chose not to fight his way through. Instead, he set up a siege, placing artillery guns, fortifications, and trenches along the Rebel line. For a month, McClellan waited to attack.

The balloons became McClellan's eye in the sky. Although April's weather was rainy, on most days Thaddeus Lowe and James Allen took up the balloons several times. When the aeronauts ascended alone, they reported to army commanders after landing, using maps to point out what they'd seen from the air.

But usually Lowe and Allen went up with army officers, mapmakers, and engineers, because many military leaders didn't trust the aeronauts to give reliable reports. Union officer George Armstrong Custer later revealed the widespread army opinion that "it was to the interest of the aeronauts to magnify their statements and render their own importance greater, thereby insuring themselves what might be profitable employment. ..." Even General Fitz John Porter, who supported the Balloon Corps, believed that only a military-trained observer was able to understand the view from the sky.

**Yorktown Siege**
James Gibson's photograph from spring 1862 shows soldiers standing next to mortars set up as part of General McClellan's siege of Yorktown, Virginia.

## SABOTAGE

The Confederates considered the balloons a threat, no matter who was on board. Whenever the Southern gunners saw a balloon launched, both the balloon and its launch site became targets. The gunners often shot dozens of shells. The missed shots ripped large branches off trees and blew huge holes in the ground.

At times the firing forced Thaddeus to shift a balloon camp to a safer location in order to protect people on the ground. Lowe wrote later, "A hawk hovering above a chicken yard could not have caused more commotion than did my balloons when they appeared before Yorktown."

One day during the siege when Thaddeus and General Porter were up in a balloon, the Confederates opened a barrage of fire from their artillery guns. A shell whizzed through the cords holding the basket to the envelope. It landed on the ground near General McClellan, who was watching the ascension. Another shell hit a tent with two soldiers inside.

A member of the balloon crew wrote in his diary that as soon as the balloon rose, "the shells began to come[,] you better believe, one shot came within three feet of my head, I don't like the fun, it is not pretty."

No one was injured that day. But the shooting was so intense that Porter ordered Lowe to take the balloon down before stray shells killed anyone.

The Confederates were willing to try anything to stop the spy balloons. According to one Southern soldier's account after the war, the Rebels offered a reward to anyone who blew up a balloon on the ground. "I was promised $1,000 in gold," he claimed, "and a commission as a second lieutenant if I succeeded. ..."

Five Rebels tried. One even posed as a peddler and visited the balloon camp. But the camp was well guarded, and he failed. Lowe later reported that three of the five

men were caught and shot as spies.

Another time, three dozen Rebel sharpshooters stealthily approached the Union lines at night and hid. In the morning, they planned to shoot from close up at the ascending balloon. Before they carried out their plot, Union soldiers captured or killed most of them.

**Thaddeus Lowe,** when he was in his thirties.

## THE REBELS RETREAT

On the first Saturday night in May 1862, a month after the Union siege at Yorktown started, the Confederate artillery began a steady, intense bombardment of Union positions. Later that night, the shelling mysteriously stopped. At dawn, one of the generals ordered Lowe to take him up in the *Intrepid* to find out what was going on.

Not a single Rebel soldier remained. The Confederates had abandoned their positions in the dark of night. Thaddeus and the general saw the enemy troops in the distance, heading up the peninsula.

Confederate general Joseph Johnston had watched the Union build up its forces only a few hundred yards away from his defenses. He knew the Rebels didn't have the men or weapons to stop the Army of the Potomac. Instead of losing his army in a fight, Johnston ordered a retreat. And the Rebels slipped away from General McClellan again.

**General Joseph E. Johnston (1807–91)**
Johnston was born in Virginia and graduated from the U.S. Military Academy at West Point, a classmate of the Confederate general Robert E. Lee. He served in the U.S. Army for more than thirty years until April 1861, when he resigned to join the Confederacy.

# Confederate Spy Balloons

The first time the Confederates used a spy balloon was in mid-April 1862 during the Peninsula Campaign in Virginia. The cotton balloon was inflated on the ground with hot air produced by burning pine knots and turpentine. Anchored by a single long rope, the balloon twirled around in the air, making observations difficult. It was leaky and stayed aloft only for a few hours.

Captain John Randolph Bryan, age twenty-one, volunteered to go up in the balloon. He ascended three times near Yorktown, drawing maps of Union positions. Yankee soldiers shot at the balloon as soon as it appeared above the trees.

Lowe saw the Confederate balloon and predicted "it would burst or fall apart after a week." He was almost right.

Three weeks later, Captain Bryan made his last ascent. As the balloon rose from the ground, a soldier's leg became tangled in the anchor rope. To free the man, the ground crew cut the rope. The wind blew away the untethered balloon—with Bryan still in the basket.

After drifting over Union lines and almost crashing in the York River, Bryan came down safely within Confederate territory. Historians don't know if the balloon was ever used again.

By late June 1862, the Confederate generals had acquired a better balloon, this one made of silk. Confederate general James Longstreet wrote an account in 1886 in which he claimed that the balloon had been made from "all the silk dresses in the Confederacy." That led to the myth of a "silk dress balloon."

Actually, the balloon was built in Savannah, Georgia, from dress fabric bought from local merchants by Confederate officer Langdon Cheves. The brightly colored plaids and flower patterns of the silk material made the *Gazelle* look like a beautiful patchwork.

Near the end of June 1862, Cheves delivered the balloon to Richmond, where General Robert E. Lee faced the Union army. Lee immediately put Lieutenant Colonel E. P. Alexander in charge of the balloon and directed him to spy on Union positions.

Alexander filled the *Gazelle* with coal gas at the Richmond Gas Works. The silk balloon wasn't much better at holding gas than the cotton one, and it stayed high in the sky for just three or four hours. Since the *Gazelle* could lift only one passenger, Alexander went up alone. He didn't use the telegraph as the Union aeronauts did. Instead, he signaled information to officers on the ground using black canvas balls that hung below the basket.

Throughout the Seven Days Battles (June 25–July 1, 1862), the Confederates used the balloon day and night. When the Union army retreated toward the James River, Alexander made balloon observations tethered to a boat in the river. This proved to be the end of the *Gazelle*. The boat soon ran aground, and a Union gunboat captured it—and the balloon. Alexander escaped. Confederate general Longstreet called the capture of the balloon "the meanest trick of the war and one I have never yet forgiven."

After the loss of the *Gazelle*, Southern balloonist Charles Cevor built another multicolored silk balloon, the *Nimbus*. Starting in the fall of 1862, he made observations along the South Carolina coast. But less than a year later, the balloon, unmanned, blew away and was captured by Union troops.

That was the last of the Confederate balloons. As the war continued, the South lacked the money to build more. Its leaky balloons had never worked as well as the Union's. Since the Confederates had no portable hydrogen gas generators, the balloons had to be inflated with city gas, which limited where they could be used.

One of the captured Confederate silk balloons—which one is not clear—was taken to Washington. It was cut into pieces and passed out to government officials as a trophy of war. Thaddeus Lowe received a section of the captured balloon, too. He kept it for the rest of his life as a souvenir of his Balloon Corps days.

## Edward Porter Alexander (1835–1910)

Born in Georgia, E. P. Alexander was trained as an engineer at the U.S. Military Academy at West Point. He served with the U.S. Army until the Civil War broke out, when he signed on with the Confederate army. During the war, he was involved in artillery and signaling operations as well as intelligence gathering.

CHAPTER SIX

# Into Battle

After the Rebels retreated to Richmond, Thaddeus took up a balloon to see which path they were taking. Union forces pursued the Confederates up the peninsula, slowly trudging over roads turned into deep mud by heavy rains. The Balloon Corps went upriver on the balloon boat *Custis*, moving three of its balloons along with generators and supplies. The aeronauts periodically ascended from the boat's deck as they traveled.

By late May, the Balloon Corps was operating from two camps in Virginia a few miles apart. One was in a wheat field at the Gaines farm on a hill above the Chickahominy River. The other was on the Cosby farm a mile from the town of Mechanicsville. The aeronauts were within ten miles of Richmond. From the air, Lowe could "look into the windows of the city of Richmond" and hear church bells ringing.

The area between the Chickahominy River and Richmond was filled with Confederate camps and fortifications. General McClellan believed his army was outnumbered, and he waited for reinforcements before moving against the enemy. The extra troops never came. President Lincoln held them back to guard Washington, because he was afraid to leave the capital exposed to attack. So once again, General McClellan set up a siege.

The Balloon Corps was ordered to ascend "as frequently as is practicable" and to give General McClellan's nearby headquarters the "full reports of the results of the observations. ..." With the Rebels shooting at them, Lowe and James Allen went up in the balloons as often as a dozen times a day from different locations. From the sky, the aeronauts spotted enemy camps and artillery batteries hidden from ground view.

**Richmond, Virginia**
The Confederate capital in 1862. The capitol building is visible on the distant hill. From the balloon, the aeronauts had a clear view of the city's church steeples.

They took up army officers, who analyzed the Rebel defenses and directed cannon fire against it.

Virginia's spring rains continued. Rivers and streams rose higher, mud grew deeper, and soldiers became more miserable. On stormy days, the balloons couldn't operate.

Thaddeus did not waste his free time. When he wasn't taking up army officers, he gave rides to reporters and artists eager to get a look at the Confederate capital. He was an expert at generating publicity for himself and promoting the Balloon Corps.

Lowe's love of attention earned him a reputation among the troops. A New York soldier wrote about the Balloon Corps in his journal: "Swell trains carrying inflators, 100 men at his [Lowe's] disposal, hand and glove state of amity with Little Mac [General McClellan], fine cloth coats and little boots (so as not to weigh down the balloon, I suppose), handsome horses, wall tents, and commander in chief of Balloon Department of the Army of the Potomac!! Fine high position whether up or down, is it not?"

## BATTLE OF FAIR OAKS/SEVEN PINES*
### May 31–June 1, 1862

On May 29, while he dangled in his basket beneath the balloon, Thaddeus noticed Confederate troops concentrating in one area across the Chickahominy River. He immediately reported from his camp at the Gaines farm that "the enemy … seem to be strengthening on our left, opposite this place."

General McClellan responded by moving up reserve troops to be ready in case the Rebels attacked.

Two days later, in the early afternoon of May 31, Lowe ascended in the *Excelsior* from the Mechanicsville camp. He spotted Confederate infantry and cavalry on the roads approaching Union troops on the Richmond side of the Chickahominy. The Rebels were about to strike a third of McClellan's army!

*The Union army called the battle "Fair Oaks," and the Confederates, "Seven Pines."

**Lowe's Balloon Camp**
This photograph of the *Constitution* at the balloon camp near the Chickahominy River, Virginia, was taken in late May 1862, probably by James Gibson. Lowe traveled between balloon launch sites by horseback.

**The Battle of Fair Oaks**
In this Currier and Ives print, a Union balloon (upper left corner) looks down on the intense fighting on May 31, 1862.

The Chickahominy River was usually a narrow stream. But a thunderstorm the night before had flooded it and washed out most of the Union's temporary bridges. From his bird's-eye view, Lowe saw that the swollen river cut these Union troops off from reinforcements on the other side.

Thaddeus was desperate to report to the generals what he was seeing from the air. Lowe needed the *Intrepid*, a balloon with more lifting power than the smaller *Excelsior*. Using the larger balloon, he could carry up a telegraph operator with the equipment to send messages quickly.

Mounting his horse, Thaddeus rode six miles to the balloon camp at the Gaines farm. The crew there was filling the *Intrepid*, but the gas generator would not finish the inflation for another hour. That was too long for Lowe to wait. "As I saw the two armies coming nearer and nearer together," Thaddeus wrote later, "there was no time to be lost."

**An Emergency Inflation**
During the Battle of Fair Oaks, Lowe quickly inflated the *Intrepid* by using a cooking kettle to transfer hydrogen gas from the *Constitution* (lying on the ground). In this photograph taken by James Gibson, the transfer is nearly complete. Lowe stands in the foreground in a black hat.

The *Constitution* was already filled with gas. But it was too small to lift both Thaddeus and a telegraph operator. The aeronaut had trained his balloon crews in a technique to transfer gas from one balloon to another, which they occasionally used to save time. Now Lowe tried an even faster method. He grabbed a cooking kettle lying on the ground and had one of his crew cut out its bottom. Using the kettle, he connected the two balloons. The hydrogen gas rapidly flowed from the smaller balloon into the larger one. Within five minutes, the *Intrepid* was ready.

Thaddeus and the telegraph operator ascended to a thousand feet in the *Intrepid*. Telegraph wires connected it directly to General McClellan's headquarters and to Fort Monroe.

Meanwhile, General McClellan had ordered Union troops to fix the flooded bridges and cross the Chickahominy River. They were to relieve the cornered troops at the Seven Pines crossroads and Fair Oaks Station along the railroad.

Throughout the rest of the day, Thaddeus watched the conflict through field glasses. The telegraph operator relayed Lowe's messages about the battle's progress. Officers who later went up with the men telegraphed Union artillerists of the exact location of Rebel cannons so that the gunners could hit them. By late afternoon, the Union reinforcements crossed the river in time to prevent a crushing defeat by the Confederates.

The battle resumed the next morning, June 1. Lowe received orders to keep two balloons up all day and to send messages about the action to headquarters every fifteen minutes. He launched from the Gaines farm, and James Allen operated at the Cosby farm near Mechanicsville.

The fighting was fierce. Clouds of blue and white smoke from muskets and artillery hung over the battlefield. Although he was high above the ground, Thaddeus clearly heard the screams and shouts of soldiers and the roar and bang of their weapons.

**The Grapevine Bridge Over the Chickahominy River**
A few days before the Battle of Fair Oaks, soldiers from New Hampshire built this bridge. It connected the two parts of the Union army separated by the river. The night before the battle, torrential rains caused flooding. Lowe nervously watched from his balloon as soldiers struggled to cross the unstable bridge in time to relieve troops under attack on the other side of the river. By the next morning, the bridge had washed away. The photograph was taken by D. B. Woodbury, and the glass negative from which it was made later cracked.

Lowe received telegraphed messages from General McClellan's headquarters. One read, "Can you see [Union] General Sumner's corps near the line of railroad about four miles from the Chickahominy?"

Thaddeus scanned the scene below with his field glasses. He sent the message that General Sumner's troops were "near the line of railroad, but not more than two miles from the Chickahominy."

Lowe's reports that day reached President Lincoln, who read the messages as they came into the War Department telegraph office. According to one witness, "Old Abe ... was very blue ... when news came of the repulse of the left wing on the Chickahominy, but got better the next day when the balloon man telegraphed every few minutes how Kearny [Union general Philip Kearny] was driving back the foe and recovering our lost ground. ..."

By noon, the fighting had ended. Lowe sent the message that the Confederates were retreating toward Richmond. From the balloon, he watched a long line of Confederate ambulances and wagons carrying the dead and wounded from the battlefield on the road to Richmond. That evening he reported, "Camp-fires around Richmond as usual, showing that the enemy are back."

The battle had no clear victor, and both sides suffered about the same number of casualties. But the Union had held its positions along the Chickahominy River.

## DAILY REPORTS

Although the fighting was brutal, many soldiers died that spring and summer from disease, not bullets. The unusually wet and stormy weather in the swampy peninsula led to outbreaks of typhoid fever, dysentery, and malaria. One-tenth of each army was sick. Thaddeus Lowe and James Allen both felt ill, but they continued their observations.

Throughout June, the Balloon Corps watched as the Confederates brought in more troops and strengthened Richmond's defenses. Using three balloons, the aeronauts made flights at all hours of the day and night, often ascending a dozen times a day. Rising as high as two thousand feet, they took up officers and mapmakers.

Lowe and Allen also filed their own dispatches about artillery and camp locations. In one typical message, Lowe wrote, "Two sections of a battery, of three guns each, are stationed in the field (with horses attached) about three-quarters of a mile southeast from Doctor Garnett's house."

The Balloon Corps reports added to the intelligence that General McClellan received from scouts and spies on the ground. In mid-June, the general informed the secretary of war that "the enemy are intrenching, daily increasing in numbers, and determined to fight desperately."

The Richmond newspapers regularly mentioned the balloons. They floated so close to the Confederate capital that the Southerners could make out the names and designs.

**Lowe Writes a Dispatch**
A crew of Union soldiers holds down the balloon while Thaddeus Lowe stands in the basket writing his report. The messenger on horseback waits to take the dispatch to the commanding general. If Lowe did not ascend with a telegraph operator, he often wrote out his messages after landing. At other times, he wrote his report while in the air, attached it to a ring, and slid it down an anchor cable. From lower heights, he wrapped the paper around a rock and dropped it to the ground, or he simply shouted down to a telegraph operator or messenger.

In a letter to his uncle from a Rebel camp along the Chickahominy River, a soldier from Georgia wrote, "Since the battle of the [May]31$^s$ and [June]1$^{st}$, the Yankees have made no demonstrations for a general fight. They are however active—sending up Balloons all along our lines—building bridges and shelling our camps with their long range guns."

To check whether Confederate gunners were aiming *their* long-range rifles and cannons at the balloons, Lowe's crews sometimes first launched a balloon with an empty basket or man-decoy. One crew member wrote that "when she [the balloon] was up 500 feet a shot come whissing over head & when we was pulling her down, thire was another struck within 30 paces of one snatch block. ..."

Union soldiers bet on whether the Southern artillerists would make a hit. The Rebel shots never brought down a balloon, but shell fragments occasionally nicked a basket or the cords. The aeronauts bravely ignored the danger, and the balloon crews grew accustomed to the fire.

## SEVEN DAYS BATTLES
### June 25–July 1, 1862

The Confederate commanders had not been idle while the Army of the Potomac waited along the Chickahominy River. After General Joseph Johnston was wounded during the Battle of Fair Oaks, Robert E. Lee became commander of the Army of Northern Virginia. Lee sent for more troops and planned a new assault to push the Union forces back from Richmond.

Lee struck on June 26. That day Lowe launched a balloon from General McClellan's headquarters. He reported a large force of Rebels crossing the Chickahominy River and attacking Union positions near Mechanicsville. Thaddeus was ordered to stay in the air, but the smoke from the battle was sometimes so dense that he saw very little.

Early the next morning, June 27, he reported, "I am very unwell. ..." Although still suffering from fever, Thaddeus stayed in the balloon, sending his observations to headquarters by messenger. He watched the horrific scene at Gaines's Mill as shells exploded and shrapnel tore into bodies. He saw lines of soldiers, puffs of smoke bursting from their muskets. He spotted men charging forward on horses. He heard thundering artillery guns.

"About two miles and a half from the river, in an open field," Lowe reported, "there are large bodies of troops. … On the field near where [Union] General Morell was camped everything is on fire. … I should judge that the enemy might make an attack on our left at any moment."

In later years, Lowe claimed that his observations that day caused Union officers to move reserves, saving many troops from capture. Others had a different opinion. A soldier from North Carolina wrote in his diary, "I do not think that their balloons did them much good."

After the third day of battle, General McClellan decided the enemy was going to cut off his army from its supply line. He ordered a withdrawal to Harrison's Landing on the James River. Having come as close as five miles from Richmond, the Union army pulled back.

With the Confederates in pursuit of Union forces, the Balloon Corps packed up its equipment. In the dark on Saturday, June 28, the crew emptied out the gas from the last balloon and joined the long wagon train retreating to the James River. The men had not traveled far when one of their wagons broke down.

## Robert E. Lee (1807–70)

Lee was born in Virginia and graduated at age twenty-two from the U.S. Military Academy at West Point. He served in the U.S. Army Corps of Engineers for more than thirty years, including three years as the superintendent of West Point. When the Civil War broke out and Virginia seceded from the Union, Lee chose to fight with the Confederacy. By January 1865, he had become general in chief of the Confederate army. He surrendered to General Ulysses S. Grant on April 9, 1865, ending the Civil War.

Eleven days later, photographer Mathew Brady arranged to take several pictures of Lee by the back door of his Richmond home. Brady and Lee must not have noticed the graffiti scribbled five bricks above the chair. The word *Devil* was written probably by a Union soldier or sympathizer after Richmond fell to Northern troops. The graffiti appears in this photograph but was rubbed out in other pictures taken that day.

Knowing that the Rebels were close behind, the crew was ready to burn the balloon on board rather than have it captured. Fortunately, another wagon arrived in time and carried the balloon to safety.

In the hasty retreat, the Balloon Corps had to leave behind three generators and the iron and acid supplies. The Confederates found them but were never able to use the materials for their own balloon.

Burning with fever, Thaddeus went back to his home and family in Philadelphia to recover from his illness. He left James Allen in charge of the Balloon Corps. His father, Clovis, helped Allen manage and maintain the balloons, and Allen arranged for one of Thaddeus's soldier brothers to join Clovis on the crew. In late July, aeronaut John Steiner returned from his duty on the Mississippi River to make ascensions with Allen.

James Allen kept Thaddeus informed. "We had two of the hottest days I ever

**Battle of Gaines's Mill**
This sketch was drawn by Prince de Joinville, a French nobleman accompanying his two nephews while they served under General McClellan. Union general Fitz John Porter, sitting tallest on his black horse, gives orders. During this battle, a surprised Thaddeus Lowe spotted Confederate officer E. P. Alexander as both men hovered above the ground in balloons. Lowe reported to Union headquarters, "About four miles to the west from here the enemy have a balloon about 300 feet in the air."

**Savage's Station, Along the Railroad on the Virginia Peninsula**
During the last days of the Seven Days Battles, the Union field hospital at Savage's Station was crowded with wounded and sick soldiers. The Army of the Potomac was retreating to the James River, and the Confederates were following. Most of the men in this photograph were left behind, along with about three thousand others who were too injured to walk. They were captured when the Rebels arrived on June 29. This famous photograph was taken by James Gibson on June 27.

witnessed while the Excellsior was inflated," he wrote in a letter, "and when I took her down[,] the cement was just the same as when I inflated, so I am satisfied with the valves."

Launching balloons from land and boat, the Balloon Corps kept an eye out for a Rebel attack on the Union army's base at Harrison's Landing. The attack never came.

By the end of August, the Balloon Corps and the Army of the Potomac had abandoned the Virginia peninsula. After five months and tens of thousands of casualties, General McClellan's army had failed to fire a single shot into the Confederate capital.

Historians disagree about whether the aeronauts' observations were helpful to the Union during the spring and summer of 1862. General McClellan seemed to think they were. In his official report, he wrote, "To Professor Lowe, the intelligent and enterprising aeronaut, who had the management of the balloons, I was greatly indebted for the valuable information obtained during his ascensions."

CHAPTER SEVEN

# The Final Conflict

By early September 1862, the Balloon Corps was back at its home base in Washington. Thaddeus Lowe had recovered from his fever and was ready to lead the corps again. After the Peninsula Campaign, however, the Union army had reorganized. It took Lowe a couple of weeks to find someone in command who would give the Balloon Corps orders to rejoin the army.

While he waited, the two enemies met in mid-September at the bloody Battle of Antietam in western Maryland. Thaddeus was sure the balloons could have helped the Union army crush the outnumbered Confederates. Instead, the defeated Rebels managed to escape back to Virginia.

Even the Confederates seemed surprised that the balloons hadn't been used. Confederate officer E. P. Alexander later wrote that "the open character of the country would have often exposed … the most important movements of the Confederates, had balloonists been on the lookout."

After the battle, Lowe finally received orders to take the balloons up the Potomac River to Sharpsburg, Maryland, and join the Union forces. Throughout October, the aeronauts made ascensions to observe Confederate activity in the area. By then, there was little to see.

When Lowe told General McClellan about his trouble receiving travel orders, the general promised to recommend that the Balloon Corps be made a separate branch of the army. Then Lowe would have the power to move the balloons on his own. It never happened. President Lincoln and many others criticized McClellan for not chasing the Confederates when they retreated after the Battle of Antietam. In early November, Lincoln stripped McClellan of his command of the Army of the Potomac.

The change in leadership to General Ambrose Burnside created a problem for Thaddeus. He had to convince the new general of the balloons' value. Lowe wrote a letter, detailing for Burnside what the Balloon Corps could do for the army. The general was persuaded. He ordered the Balloon Corps to join the Army of the Potomac on its next campaign.

The Union plan was to attack Richmond from the north before Lee's army moved south to protect its capital. The Army of the Potomac would approach through Fredericksburg, Virginia, a town on the Rappahannock River halfway between Washington and Richmond.

By early December, the Balloon Corps had traveled to Fredericksburg. The crew set up camp across from the town, a mile from the river. Lowe brought along aeronauts James and Ezra Allen as well as his father and John O'Donnell as assistants.

## THE BATTLE OF FREDERICKSBURG
### December 11–13, 1862

The first step in the march to Richmond was to take Fredericksburg, which was guarded by a small

**General Ambrose Burnside (1824–81)**
Burnside was commander of the Army of the Potomac from November 1862 to January 1863. After the war, Burnside went into business and served as Rhode Island's governor and senator. The word *sideburns* was originally coined to describe Burnside's unusual whiskers.

**Crossing the Rappahannock River**
The Union army used these pontoon bridges to cross the river in its attack on Fredericksburg. Timothy O'Sullivan took this photograph of Northern soldiers standing by the river in late spring 1863.

Confederate force. The Union army had to cross the Rappahannock River to invade the town. The river was too wide to cross without bridges, and the Rebels had destroyed all of them.

General Burnside sent for pontoon bridges, but he had to wait almost two weeks for their delivery. By the time they arrived, thousands of Confederate forces under General Robert E. Lee had marched to Fredericksburg to halt the Union advance.

While Burnside adjusted his plans, the aeronauts waited. The general did not want to reveal to the enemy that he had the balloons until Union troops crossed the river. Perhaps Burnside feared that the Rebels might camouflage their positions if they knew the sky spies were watching.

Finally, on the morning of December 11, Burnside's troops began to lay the pontoon bridges across the icy Rappahannock River. To stop the Confederates from shooting at the men on the bridges, Union artillery bombarded the town.

When the bridges were finished later in the day, Northern troops crossed the river and occupied Fredericksburg. By then, Rebel shooters and most of the residents had been chased away. Confederate troops looked down on the town from the hills behind it and waited for the Yankees to attack them.

Lowe was glad when General Burnside finally gave the order to take up the balloons two days later. In the early morning of December 13, the fog was too thick for the aeronauts to see anything. When it cleared at 10:00 a.m., Lowe launched a balloon.

**The Battle of Fredericksburg**
Alfred Waud's drawing of the battle was published in *Harper's Weekly* on January 10, 1863.

A ferocious battle was already in progress. One Rebel soldier wrote about the cannon fire: "More than two hundred guns were belching forth their sulphurous flames, filling the fields and the heavens with vicious sights and unearthly sounds … and [they] made the earth vibrate beneath the feet."

Lowe and the Allen brothers ascended throughout the day from their camp, taking up officers and sending observations to Burnside's nearby headquarters. They watched as Union troops headed toward the Rebel defenses on the hill behind Fredericksburg. At times, strong winds tossed the balloon back and forth so much that the ground crew could not manage it. Always conscious of safety, Thaddeus refused to go up again until the wind died down.

Later when Lowe was in the air again, a Confederate shell whistled toward him. Although the Rebels continued shooting at the balloon with long-range artillery, they missed every time.

But the Confederates did *not* miss the Union troops trying to climb the hill behind the town. Thousands of Northern soldiers were massacred before General Burnside called off the attack.

The beaten Army of the Potomac retreated to the other side of the Rappahannock River, where it stayed for five months.

**Town of Fredericksburg, Virginia**
Timothy O'Sullivan took this photograph across the Rappahannock River in March 1863. This is the view that the Balloon Corps and other Union soldiers had from their camps.

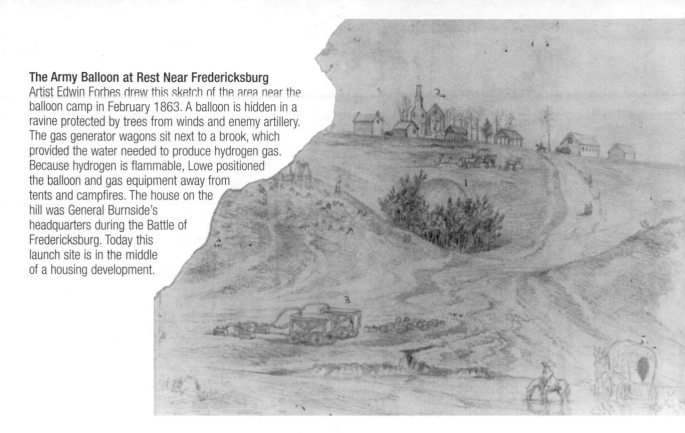

**The Army Balloon at Rest Near Fredericksburg**
Artist Edwin Forbes drew this sketch of the area near the balloon camp in February 1863. A balloon is hidden in a ravine protected by trees from winds and enemy artillery. The gas generator wagons sit next to a brook, which provided the water needed to produce hydrogen gas. Because hydrogen is flammable, Lowe positioned the balloon and gas equipment away from tents and campfires. The house on the hill was General Burnside's headquarters during the Battle of Fredericksburg. Today this launch site is in the middle of a housing development.

## WINTER WAIT

General Burnside's defeat cost him his command. Lincoln replaced him at the end of January 1863 with General Joseph Hooker, nicknamed "Fighting Joe" for his aggressiveness. Thaddeus hoped that Hooker's appointment would be good for the Balloon Corps. In fall 1861, the general had used the balloons at Budd's Ferry, Maryland, and had even gone up himself.

As the cold, damp winter dragged on, both armies waited. General Robert E. Lee and his Army of Northern Virginia waited on the southwestern side of the Rappahannock River, expecting Union troops to cross and strike again. Hooker and his Army of the Potomac waited on the opposite side, planning their attack. Rain, snow, filthy conditions, and lack of food made soldiers sick. Diseases such as measles and dysentery spread through the camps.

Lowe kept the balloons ready to make observations whenever commanders requested them, unless the winds were too strong. General Hooker wanted updates on the number and precise location of Rebel camps across the river. He ordered the aeronauts to watch the river crossings and countryside for any shifts in the enemy's positions.

**The Balloon Camp**
James Gibson shot this photograph of the Balloon Corps' tents near Fredericksburg, Virginia, probably in March 1863. The man closest to the tents appears to be Thaddeus Lowe. Gibson spent that winter with the Balloon Corps and became one of Lowe's friends.

On most days, Thaddeus and the Allens launched two or three balloons and stayed up all day. Knowing that the Rebels might try to hide their camps, the aeronauts also took up the balloons after dark and before dawn to spot campfires. They towed balloons to different locations up and down the river.

In clear weather, they saw a distance of twenty miles if they rose to two thousand feet. From the sky, the aeronauts traced the Rappahannock River winding through the landscape. They saw the lines of enemy fortifications and artillery across the river behind Fredericksburg. They noticed the haze of smoke hanging over Rebel camps toward the south. The aeronauts looked into ravines, down roads, and along streams for signs of Confederate troops and guns.

The balloons were unsettling to the Rebels. In early April, a soldier wrote his uncle in North Carolina that he could "see a man up in a balloon every day viewing our camps and we suppose they intend advancing."

Even General Robert E. Lee was concerned. He wrote one of his generals in mid-April, "The balloons are in constant observation, as if expecting or watching movement on our part."

E. P. Alexander, the colonel in charge of much of the Confederate artillery, described them as "immense black, captive balloons, like two great spirits of the air. ..."

When the Confederates shot at a balloon from across the river, the shells often fell into camps near the launch site. To avoid being hit, soldiers in one Pennsylvania regiment dashed from their tents to safety as soon as the balloon rose. One day in early February, a New Hampshire soldier was almost killed when he happened to be walking by his regiment's cesspool. A Rebel shell landed in the middle of it, drenching him in foul sewage.

During the late winter months in Fredericksburg, Thaddeus had time to test his new ideas. He realized that during a battle, officers fighting miles away often received balloon observations too late to be helpful. They did not have telegraph lines strung to their battlefield position, and messengers took too long to deliver Lowe's reports.

Thaddeus's plan was to signal his reports directly from the balloon so that officers could see them immediately with field glasses. For signals, he experimented with flags and with small hot air balloons carrying colored flares and markings on

**General Joseph Hooker (1814–79)**
Hooker fought in the Mexican-American War and in many Civil War battles before becoming commander of the Army of the Potomac in January 1863. Lincoln was not satisfied with Hooker's performance at the Battle of Chancellorsville. He replaced him with General George Meade in late June 1863, right before the Battle of Gettysburg. Hooker retired from the army in 1868.

their envelopes. Lowe wanted to test them in the next battle, but he didn't get the chance.

Unfortunately, Thaddeus was more interested in spying from the balloons and developing new methods than in properly filling out army paperwork. Displeased with Lowe's management, General Hooker's office put Captain Cyrus Comstock in charge of supervising the balloons. Comstock had been trained at West Point as an engineer, and he wanted complete control of the Balloon Corps. He went up in the balloons himself and learned how they operated.

Comstock had little respect for the aeronauts' work and abilities. Thaddeus had a low opinion of Comstock. Their relationship grew worse in early April after the captain cut Thaddeus's salary and fired his assistants, Clovis Lowe and John O'Donnell.

**The *Eagle* in a Storm**
High winds made it difficult for the crew to control a balloon. Ignoring orders from officers, Lowe refused to ascend in such unsafe conditions. In this wood engraving, a balloon crew struggles to hold down the *Eagle*.

This infuriated Lowe. He had had enough of the U.S. Army. He was tired of fighting for money to buy supplies and pay his employees. Thaddeus had a family back home to support, and he could no longer afford to do it on his reduced salary.

He complained to General Hooker's chief of staff. "I feel aggrieved that my services should not have been better appreciated," he wrote. "It will be impossible for me to serve upon any other conditions than those with which I entered the service."

With that, he resigned from the Balloon Corps. Thaddeus knew, however, that a major battle between the armies was looming. He promised to stay on—without pay—until the fighting was over.

## THE BATTLE OF CHANCELLORSVILLE
### May 1–6, 1863

As spring arrived, General Hooker planned his strike against Lee's Army of Northern Virginia. To prepare for his attack, the general ordered the Balloon Corps to learn more about the Confederates' positions and movement.

Lowe and the Allen brothers made observations from the *Washington*, tethered across the Rappahannock River from Fredericksburg, and from the *Eagle*, stationed a few miles upriver. They sent reports to General Hooker, noting where the enemy was strongest.

During the final days of April, Hooker made his move. He marched most of his troops up and across the Rappahannock and Rapidan rivers. This placed tens of thousands of Union soldiers behind Lee's army near the crossroad of Chancellorsville, about ten miles west of Fredericksburg. Hooker left the rest of his soldiers to attack the Confederate forces at Fredericksburg. He planned to squeeze the Rebels before they realized what was happening.

The Balloon Corps stayed close to Fredericksburg, watching Rebel movement around the town and along the river. The area near Chancellorsville was heavily wooded, preventing the aeronauts from seeing much there.

On Friday morning, May 1, the aeronauts took up the balloons to check the roads for Confederate soldiers. But heavy fog blocked their view. By the time the sky cleared in midmorning, they saw that the enemy was rapidly advancing to challenge General Hooker's troops. Lowe sent his message to the commanders: "The largest

**The Battle of Chancellorsville**
This Currier and Ives print shows an artist's idea of the mortal wounding of Thomas "Stonewall" Jackson during the Battle of Chancellorsville. Jackson, one of the Confederate army's greatest generals, was mistakenly shot on May 2 by Rebel troops. Although the Confederates won the battle, his death was considered a great military loss in the South.

column of the enemy is moving on the road toward Chancellorsville." 

Throughout the day, the aeronauts reported the locations where the Rebels were marching, digging rifle pits, and building earthworks. Union officers went up with the aeronauts to look for themselves. At midday, Lowe reported, "In a west-northwest direction, about twelve miles, an engagement is going on. Can see heavy smoke and hear artillery."

As the battle continued the next day, the aeronauts struggled to keep the balloons up in high winds. When they were able to ascend, it was often too bouncy to use their spyglasses.

Later on May 2, General Lee turned the tables on General Hooker. Lee split his Confederate troops and sent thousands of soldiers in a sneak attack on one end of the Union line. The Rebels caught Hooker by surprise.

The next morning, Lowe received orders to look for the weak spot in the Confederate lines on the hill behind Fredericksburg. Thaddeus reported from the balloon, "The enemy's infantry is very light along the whole line opposite here, and especially immediately in the rear of Fredericksburg."

By 11:00 a.m., Union troops had broken through that line and advanced west toward Chancellorsville to support Hooker. General John Sedgwick, who commanded the charge, later credited the balloons with helping him. In a letter to Lowe, he said that staff officers who ascended "obtained valuable information which could not have been procured by any other means then at my command."

The next two days, however, were a disaster for the Army of the Potomac. Because of poor decisions by the Union generals, the Confederates took Chancellorsville and recaptured Fredericksburg.

On the morning of May 5, Lowe telegraphed the bad news to Union headquarters: "The enemy in force appear to hold all the ground they gained yesterday."

By early the next day, Hooker's army had retreated to safety across the Rappahannock River, defeated by a Confederate army half its size.

With the Battle of Chancellorsville over, Thaddeus kept his vow to resign. He packed up his belongings and returned to Washington, leaving the Balloon Corps forever. His great plan for the spy balloons had not turned out the way he'd dreamed. Neither he nor the Balloon Corps ever received the respect

**Lowe's Sketch**
On May 1, 1863, Thaddeus made this pencil sketch in a small notebook he took up in his balloon. He called the drawing "Reflection of Balloon in the Dense Fog" and labeled where rainbow colors surrounded the basket.

from the U.S. Army that he felt they deserved.

After Lowe left, James and Ezra Allen continued to spy on the Rebels along the Rappahannock River. But the balloons were in poor condition after months of use. In early June, the *Washington* burst a thirty-six-foot-long seam with Ezra Allen on board. Luckily, he landed safely. The Allens tried to persuade the War Department to pay for new balloons. Their plea fell on deaf ears.

During the first half of June, the Allens saw signs that the Confederates were leaving Fredericksburg. Camps and artillery batteries had disappeared, and Rebel wagons were traveling on the roads. From the air, the Allens and Union officers spotted clouds of dust and bayonets shining in the sun. Lee's army was headed north.

The Army of the Potomac chased after them but did not take along the aeronauts. The balloons were ordered back to Washington in mid-June.

A couple of weeks later, the two armies would clash at Gettysburg, Pennsylvania, in a great battle that changed the course of the war. The Balloon Corps would not be there.

CHAPTER EIGHT

# Grounded

Thaddeus Lowe was reluctant to give up his dream. Over the next several months, he tried to convince the War Department that the Balloon Corps should be a permanent part of the military. He performed balloon demonstrations in Washington and collected complimentary letters from generals about the spy balloons. Lowe also complained to the secretary of war about the way he'd been treated during the previous two years. He claimed that the government owed him money for his wages and expenses.

Thaddeus succeeded in getting some payment, but he failed to save the Balloon Corps. The Union army never used the balloons after the summer of 1863.

Aeronauts James and Ezra Allen went on to run a balloon corps for the Brazilian army in 1867. After their war duty, they operated separate balloon businesses, traveling to fairs and carnivals throughout New England.

**A Ticket to Fly**
In 1864, a year after he had left the Balloon Corps, Lowe was in business again, advertising spectacular views of Philadelphia from heights of one hundred to a thousand feet. This ticket "to an Army Balloon Ascension" sold for five dollars. Lowe also sold closeup looks at the balloon and equipment for twenty-five cents.

**The Lowe Family**
Thaddeus and Leontine Lowe pose with their ten children in the yard of their Norristown, Pennsylvania, home in the 1880s.

Lowe eventually accepted that his spying days were over. Publicity about the Balloon Corps had made him even more famous than he was before the war. Thaddeus took advantage of it. He went into business again, presenting aerial demonstrations and giving rides in Philadelphia and New York. He used several balloons, including the *Washington* and *United States*, which he bought from the government.

Within a few years, however, Thaddeus achieved more success as an inventor than as an aeronaut. His interest in experimentation and his knowledge of chemistry led him to come up with two innovations. One was a cheaper way to produce gas for heating and lighting. This allowed smaller towns to provide gas to their citizens. The second was a method for making artificial ice to keep foods cold, before homes and businesses had refrigerators. Lowe's inventions earned him scientific honors, and the resulting businesses made him a wealthy man.

In the late 1880s, Lowe moved his family from Pennsylvania to California, a state that was growing and developing. Soon Thaddeus was involved in another ambitious project. Near Los Angeles, he built an electric railway up a mountain, on which he opened a resort for tourists and an observatory for astronomers. The mountain was later named Mount Lowe in his honor. Unfortunately, his project lost money, and Thaddeus was forced into bankruptcy, losing ownership of his properties.

Thaddeus wanted to be remembered for establishing America's first air force. He hired the chief clerk of the Smithsonian Institution to organize his war notes for a report to the government. Lowe wrote his memoirs and kept up his ties with the press. Articles and interviews about his Civil War exploits appeared throughout his lifetime and long after his death.

Over the years, military experts and historians have debated the effectiveness of Lowe's spy balloons. Some Civil War commanders did not correctly interpret or use the aerial observations, and they were unimpressed by the balloons. Other Union generals, such as George McClellan, valued them.

General George Stoneman claimed he "never made an ascent without coming down much better informed ...

**The Mount Lowe Railway in California, 1899**
Thaddeus Lowe and his partner, engineer David Macpherson, built the railway, opening it in 1893. Electric trolley cars carried passengers to scenic views, hotels, restaurants, and an astronomical observatory. Six years later, Lowe had lost ownership because of his financial problems. The railway was abandoned in 1938 after several fires and floods destroyed most of it.

than I could possibly have been by any other means." General Samuel Heintzelman, who had gone up with Lowe before and during the Peninsula Campaign, called the balloons "indispensable to an army in the field."

The spy balloons were certainly successful in threatening the Confederates. Southern officer E. P. Alexander wrote after the war, "Even if the observers never saw anything, they [the balloons] would have been worth all they cost for the annoyance and delays they caused us in trying to keep our movements out of their sight."

Despite their benefits, the balloons had drawbacks. The aeronauts could not go up in stormy weather. Fog, thick smoke, or leafy trees blocked their view of the ground. Even when the aeronauts made important observations of the enemy, the information sometimes failed to reach the commanders on the battlefield fast enough to be useful.

When the army changed location, it took time for the Balloon Corps to move deflated balloons, gas generators, and supplies. Although the balloon boat helped to

**The Siege of Paris, 1870–71**
During the four-month siege of France's capital during the Franco-Prussian War, hot air balloons carried people and mail to safety over the heads of German troops. This nineteenth-century French print shows a balloon flying past a French fort during the siege.

**Thaddeus Lowe, Retired Aeronaut**
Lowe sits in his office in Pasadena, California, where he lived the last years of his life. After he broke his hip in a fall, Lowe's health failed. He died on January 16, 1913.

transfer equipment by water, the generator wagons traveled slowly on muddy roads. For short distances, a balloon crew was able to tow an inflated balloon. But the men had to walk carefully to avoid snagging it on trees.

Keeping a balloon in one place created another problem. Because the enemy saw it bobbing in the sky, the balloon gave away the location of Union camps and made them vulnerable to Confederate shelling.

Thaddeus Lowe worked hard to overcome these shortcomings and convince others of the spy balloons' worth. In the end, though, the Balloon Corps could not survive without the support of a champion in the army like General George McClellan.

After the Civil War, the Europeans used war balloons successfully. The U.S. Army brought them back during the 1890s, and during World War I, a balloon division of the army was established. Hundreds of officers ascended in tethered balloons to spot targets, help aim artillery fire, and note the action behind the enemy's front lines. But by this time, airplanes were taking over the skies.

Thaddeus Lowe had predicted that future more than forty years before the Wright brothers flew their airplane at Kitty Hawk in 1903—a day he lived to see. "I have no doubt, but cherish a fervent hope," he wrote as a young man, "that the time is not far distant when we can travel in the air without the aid of balloons."

# TIMELINE

**1783**

SEPTEMBER 19  Flight in France of the world's first hot air balloon passengers—a sheep, rooster, and duck.

DECEMBER 1  Flight in France of the first human in a hydrogen balloon.

**1832**

AUGUST 20  Thaddeus Lowe born in Jefferson, New Hampshire.

**1846–48**

Mexican-American War.

**1855**

Thaddeus and Leontine Lowe marry in New York City.

**1856**

Lowe establishes a balloon business.

**1859–60**

Lowe plans a transatlantic balloon flight.

**1860**

NOVEMBER 6  Abraham Lincoln elected president of the United States.

**1861**

FEBRUARY  Confederate States of America formed.

MARCH 4  Abraham Lincoln inaugurated as United States president.

APRIL 12  Confederate troops fire on Fort Sumter, South Carolina, and the Civil War begins.

APRIL 20  Thaddeus Lowe flies a balloon from Ohio to South Carolina, where he is arrested for spying.

JUNE 18  Lowe sends the first air-to-ground telegram from his balloon during a demonstration in Washington, D.C.

JUNE–AUGUST  Aloft in his balloon, Lowe makes observations of Confederate positions around Washington.

JULY 21  First Battle of Bull Run fought in Virginia.

AUGUST  General George McClellan becomes commander of the Army of the Potomac. U.S. Army hires Lowe to build and fly its first spy balloon.

AUGUST 1861–JANUARY 1862  Lowe builds seven balloons for the army.

SEPTEMBER 1861–MARCH 1862  Lowe and the Balloon Corps spy on Confederate positions around Washington and along the Potomac River.

SEPTEMBER 24  Artillery fire is directed from a balloon for the first time, outside of Washington.

NOVEMBER  George McClellan becomes general in chief of the Union armies.

NOVEMBER 10  First aircraft carrier used to transport a balloon along the Potomac River.

# TIMELINE

**1862**

JANUARY–JUNE  Aeronaut John Starkweather spies from a balloon in South Carolina.

FEBRUARY–JUNE  Aeronaut John Steiner is based with a balloon along the Mississippi River.

Late MARCH  Lowe and the Balloon Corps travel to Virginia to join General McClellan and the Army of the Potomac for the Peninsula Campaign.

APRIL  Lowe and aeronaut James Allen operate balloons near Yorktown, Virginia.

APRIL–JUNE  Confederates use hot air spy balloons on the Virginia peninsula.

MAY–AUGUST  Balloon Corps operates balloons outside of Richmond, Virginia.

MAY 31–JUNE 1  Battle of Fair Oaks (also called Battle of Seven Pines) near Richmond, Virginia.

JUNE 25–JULY 1  Seven Days Battles near Richmond, Virginia.

JUNE 27  Union and Confederate balloons share the sky during Battle of Gaines's Mill on the Virginia peninsula.

AUGUST 28–30  Second Battle of Bull Run, Virginia.

SEPTEMBER 17  Battle of Antietam, Maryland.

NOVEMBER 7  Lincoln removes General McClellan as commander of the Army of the Potomac, replacing him with General Ambrose Burnside.

DECEMBER 11–13  Battle of Fredericksburg, Virginia.

**1863**

JANUARY  Lincoln replaces Burnside as commander of the Army of the Potomac with General Joseph Hooker.

JANUARY–JUNE  Balloon Corps makes balloon observations around Fredericksburg, Virginia.

APRIL  Lowe resigns as head of the Balloon Corps but stays with the army until the second week in May.

MAY 1–MAY 6  Battle of Chancellorsville, Virginia.

MAY–JUNE  Allen brothers continue balloon observations until ordered back to Washington in mid-June. Balloon Corps is disbanded.

**1865**

APRIL 9  Confederate general Robert E. Lee surrenders to Union general Ulysses S. Grant at Appomattox Court House, Virginia. The Civil War ends.

APRIL 15  President Abraham Lincoln dies in Washington from an assassin's bullet.

**1903**

DECEMBER 17  The Wright brothers make the first successful airplane flight at Kitty Hawk, North Carolina.

**1913**

JANUARY 16  Thaddeus Lowe dies in Pasadena, California, at age eighty.

# NOTES

The source of each quotation in this book is found below. The citation indicates the first words of the quotation and its document source. The sources are listed in the bibliography.

THE FOLLOWING ABBREVIATIONS ARE USED:

**LM** *Memoirs of Thaddeus S. C. Lowe.*

**OR** U.S. War Department, *The War of the Rebellion: A Compilation of the Official Records of the Union and Confederate Armies.*

**Lowe OR** "T.S.C. Lowe's Official Report," in *The War of the Rebellion: A Compilation of the Official Records of the Union and Confederate Armies*, series 3, vol. 3.

## CHAPTER ONE

"Haul in ..." and "Are you ...": quoted in Townsend, p. 98.

## CHAPTER TWO

"I saved ...": LM, p. 3.

"the greatest and best ...": LM, p. 4.

"one of the happiest ...": Wise, *A System of Aeronautics*, p. 153.

"I had often ...": LM, p. 5.

"I would not ...": quoted in LM, p 36.

"thinking [he] might ...": LM, p. 47.

"What state ...": LM, p. 43.

"Virginia": quoted in LM, p. 43.

"shot on the spot ...": quoted in LM, p. 46.

"fully convinced ...": LM, p. 65.

## CHAPTER THREE

"We had been attacked ...": Person C. Cheney, quoted in Thompson, p. 690.

"To President ...": telegram from Thaddeus Lowe to Abraham Lincoln, dated June 16, 1861, Lincoln Papers.

"I was almost ...": LM, p. 70.

"Would it not ...": letter from anonymous "Union" to Abraham Lincoln, July 6, 1861, Lincoln Papers.

"This point...": telegram from Thaddeus Lowe to Abraham Lincoln, dated June 16, 1861, Lincoln Papers.

"the map ...": telegram from Brigadier General Daniel Tyler to General Irvin McDowell, June 24, 1861, quoted in Haydon, p. 186.

"The Baloon ...": report from H. G. Williams to Brigadier General Milledge L. Bonham, July 3, 1861, Bonham Papers.

"Prof. Lowe ...": *Richmond Daily Dispatch*, June 27, 1861.

"the infernal ...": OR, series 1, vol. 5, p. 982.

"Neither [John Wise nor John La Mountain] ...": LM, p. 73.

"Show [your] ...": quoted in Lowe OR, p. 258.

"General ...": quoted in LM, p. 75.

## CHAPTER FOUR

"with treasonable ...": OR, series 2, vol. 2, p. 312.

"During my observations ...": Lowe OR, p. 262.

"the Federals ...": Longstreet, *From Manassas to Appomattox: Memoirs of the Civil War in America*, p. 60.

"We sent ...": letter from E. P. Alexander to A. L. Alexander, September 8, 1861, quoted in Haydon, p. 204.

"During the time ..." and "If we fire ...": Lowe OR, p. 263.

"Gen. McClellan ...": "News of the Day," *New York Times*, September 9, 1861.

"You are of value ...": Lowe OR, p. 261.

# NOTES

"I have now …": Lowe OR, p. 266.

"We had a fine …": same as above.

"As soon as …": letter from Benjamin Stevens to his parents, November 30, 1861, Stevens Papers.

"Mr. Paullin …": report from Colonel William Small to General Joseph Hooker, December 9, 1861, quoted in Haydon, p. 356.

"I am satisfyde …": letter from John Steiner to Thaddeus Lowe, June 9, 1862, quoted in Haydon, p. 392.

"I am glad …": OR, series 1, vol. 10, p. 769.

"more smokes …": Lowe OR, p. 271.

## CHAPTER FIVE

"The Most Shot-At Man …": Sandburg, p. 493.

"On to Richmond": "The Order Onward!", *New York Times*, March 17, 1862.

"glistened …": quoted in Hays, p. 76.

"The balloon …": OR, series 1, vol. 11, p. 74.

"Balloons have been …": OR, series 1, vol. 11, p. 425.

"O-pen …": quoted in Townsend, p. 93.

"I remained seated …", "one or both of us …", and "magnificent scenery": Custer, p. 158.

"I found it difficult …": Lowe OR, p. 274.

"I am just …": letter from George McClellan to Mary Ellen McClellan, April 11, 1862, *The Civil War Papers of George B. McClellan*, p. 235.

"it was to the interest …": Custer, p. 156.

"A hawk …": LM, p. 113.

"the shells began …": Tufts Diary, May 3, 1862.

"I was promised …": from the *Detroit Free Press*, 1886, quoted in LM, p. 114.

"it would burst …": quoted in Townsend, p. 92.

"all the silk …": Longstreet, "Our March Against Pope," p. 513.

"the meanest trick …": same as above.

## CHAPTER SIX

"look into …": Lowe, "The Balloons with the Army of the Potomac," p. 374.

"as frequently …" and "full reports …": Lowe OR, p. 278.

"Swell trains …": Dodge, p. 22.

"the enemy …": Lowe OR, p. 280.

"As I saw …": Lowe, "The Balloons with the Army of the Potomac," p. 375.

"Can you see …": Lowe OR, p. 282.

"near the line …": Lowe OR, p. 283.

"Old Abe …": letter from Henry A. Wise to Hamilton Fish, June 4, 1862, quoted in Nevins, p. 84.

"Camp-fires …": Lowe OR, p. 283.

"Two sections …": Lowe OR, p. 286.

"the enemy …": OR, series 1, vol. 11, p. 48.

"Since the battle …": letter from George Davison to James Nisbet, June 8, 1862, Nisbet Papers.

"when she [the balloon] was up …": Tufts Diary, June 19, 1862.

"I am very …": Lowe OR, p. 290.

"About two miles and a half …": same as above.

"I do not think …": diary of John Wetmore Hinsdale, June 27, 1862, vol. 2, p. 37, Hinsdale Papers.

"We had two …": letter from James Allen to Thaddeus Lowe, July 12, 1862, Lowe Papers, box 83.

# NOTES

"About four miles ...": Lowe OR, p. 290.

"To Professor Lowe ...": OR, series 1, vol. 5, p. 32.

## CHAPTER SEVEN

"the open character ...": Alexander, *Military Memoirs of a Confederate*, p. 288.

"More than two hundred ...": Scharf, pp. 55–56.

"see a man ...": letter from G. W. Poindexter to John F. Poindexter, April 2, 1863, Poindexter Papers.

"The balloons ...": OR, series 1, vol. 25, p. 730.

"immense black ...": Alexander, *Fighting for the Confederacy*, p. 171.

"I feel aggrieved ...": LM, p. 171.

"The largest column ...": Lowe OR, p. 313.

"In a west-northwest direction ...": same as above.

"The enemy's infantry ...": Lowe OR, p. 315.

"obtained valuable ...": letter from General John Sedgwick to Thaddeus Lowe, September 3, 1863, Lowe Papers, box 84.

"The enemy in force ...": Lowe OR, p. 316.

## CHAPTER EIGHT

"never made ...": letter from General George Stoneman to Thaddeus Lowe, July 10, 1863, Lowe Papers, box 84.

"indispensable ...": letter from General Samuel Heintzelman to Thaddeus Lowe, July 1, 1863, Lowe Papers, box 84.

"Even if the observers ...": Alexander, "The Great Charge and Artillery Fighting at Gettysburg," p. 358.

"I have no doubt ...": Lowe, "The Air-Ship City of New York: A Full Description of the Air-Ship and the Apparatus to be Employed in the Aerial Voyage to Europe," Lowe Papers, box 81.

# BIBLIOGRAPHY

Alexander, E. P. *Fighting for the Confederacy: The Personal Recollections of General Edward Porter Alexander*. Edited by Gary W. Gallagher. Chapel Hill: University of North Carolina Press, 1989.

_____. "The Great Charge and Artillery Fighting at Gettysburg." In *Battles and Leaders of the Civil War: Being for the Most Part Contributions of Union and Confederate Officers*. Vol. 3. New York: Century Co., 1888.

_____. *Military Memoirs of a Confederate: A Critical Narrative*. New York: Charles Scribner's Sons, 1907.

Anthis, Judith, and Richard M. McMurry. "Rebels in the Sky: The Confederate Balloon Corps." *Blue & Gray Magazine*, August 1991, 20–24.

Block, Eugene B. *Above the Civil War: The Story of Thaddeus Lowe, Balloonist, Inventor, Railway Builder*. Berkeley, CA: Howell-North Books, 1966.

Bonham, Milledge L. Papers. Special Collections Library, Duke University, Durham, NC.

Bruce, Robert V. *Lincoln and the Tools of War*. Indianapolis: Bobbs-Merrill, 1956.

Burton, Brian K. *The Peninsula and Seven Days*. Lincoln: University of Nebraska Press, 2007.

Buswell, Brigham. "A Sharpshooter's Seven Days." *Civil War Times*, February 1996, 20–28.

Butler, Benjamin F. *Private and Official Correspondence of Gen. Benjamin F. Butler During the Period of the Civil War, Vol. 1, April 1860–June 1862*. Norwood, MA: Plimpton Press, 1917.

Catton, Bruce. *Never Call Retreat*. New York: Washington Square Press, 1965.

_____. *Terrible Swift Sword: The Centennial History of the Civil War*. Vol. 2. Garden City, NY: Doubleday, 1963.

Confederate States of America. *Southern History of the War: Official Reports of Battles, as published by order of the Confederate Congress at Richmond*. New York: Charles B. Richardson, 1864.

Cornish, Joseph Jenkins, III. *The Air Arm of the Confederacy*. Richmond, VA: Richmond Civil War Centennial Committee, 1963.

Crouch, Tom D. *The Eagle Aloft: Two Centuries of the Balloon in America*. Washington, DC: Smithsonian Institution Press, 1983.

Custer, George Armstrong. "In the Air above Yorktown." In *Battles and Leaders of the Civil War*. Vol. 5. Edited by Peter Cozzens. Urbana: University of Illinois Press, 2002, 154–170.

Davis, Captain Daniel T. "The Air Role in the War Between the States: the Civil War balloon activities of Professor Thaddeus S.C. Lowe." *Air University Review*, July–August 1976, 13–29.

Dodge, Theodore Ayrault. *On Campaign with the Army of the Potomac: The Civil War Journal of Theodore Ayrault Dodge*. Edited by Stephen W. Sears. New York: Cooper Square Press, 2001.

Early, Jubal Anderson. *War Memoirs: Autobiographical Sketch and Narrative of the War Between the States*. Edited by Frank E. Vandiver. Bloomington: Indiana University Press, 1960.

Eicher, David J. *The Longest Night: A Military History of the Civil War*. New York: Simon and Schuster, 2001.

# BIBLIOGRAPHY

Evans, Charles M. *The War of the Aeronauts: A History of Ballooning During the Civil War.* Mechanicsburg, PA: Stackpole Books, 2002.

Evans, George C. *History of the Town of Jefferson, New Hampshire, 1773–1927.* Manchester, NH: Granite State Press, 1927.

Fanton, Ben. "View from above the Battlefield." *America's Civil War,* September 2001, 22–29.

Fishel, Edwin C. *The Secret War for the Union: The Untold Story of Military Intelligence in the Civil War.* Boston: Houghton Mifflin, 1996.

Foote, Shelby. *The Civil War, A Narrative: Fredericksburg to Meridian.* New York: Random House, 1963.

Gallagher, Gary W., ed. *The Richmond Campaign of 1862: The Peninsula and the Seven Days.* Chapel Hill: University of North Carolina Press, 2000.

Gardner, Alexander. *Gardner's Photographic Sketch Book of the Civil War.* New York: Dover Publications, 1959.

Gluba, Gregory. "Five Hundred Acres of History: Freestone Point, Virginia, in the Civil War." *Prologue* 31, no. 3 (Fall 1999): 196–199.

Gorman, Michael D. "Lee the 'Devil' Discovered at Image of War Seminar." *The Center for Civil War Photography Newsletter,* February 2006. www.civilwarphotography.org.

Greeley, General A. W. "Balloons in War." *Harper's New Monthly Magazine,* June 1900, Vol. 101, 33–50.

Hallion, Richard P. *Taking Flight: Inventing the Aerial Age from Antiquity through the First World War.* New York: Oxford University Press, 2003.

*Harper's Weekly.* "A Balloon Reconnoissance." October 26, 1861, 687.

———. "Transatlantic Ballooning." September 24, 1859, 609–610.

Hattaway, Herman. "Balloons: America's First Air Force." *American History Illustrated,* June 1984, 24–29.

Haydon, F. Stansbury. *Aeronautics in the Union and Confederate Armies, with a Survey of Military Aeronautics Prior to 1861.* Vol. 1. Baltimore: Johns Hopkins Press, 1941.

Hays, Gilbert Adams, comp. *Under the Red Patch: Story of the Sixty Third Regiment Pennsylvania Volunteers 1861–1864.* Pittsburgh: Sixty-third Pennsylvania Volunteers Regimental Association, 1908.

Henig, Gerald S., and Eric Niderost. *Civil War Firsts: The Legacies of America's Bloodiest Conflict.* Mechanicsburg, PA: Stackpole Books, 2001.

Henry, Joseph. Letter to Lowe. In "Aerial Navigation." *The Scientific American,* December 14, 1861, 373.

Hinsdale family. Papers. Special Collections Library, Duke University, Durham, NC.

# BIBLIOGRAPHY

Hoehling, Mary. *Thaddeus Lowe: America's One-Man Air Corps*. New York: Julian Messner, Inc., 1958.

Josephy, Alvin M., Jr., ed. *The American Heritage History of Flight*. New York: American Heritage Publishing, 1962.

Kagan, Neil, ed. *Eyewitness to the Civil War: The Complete History from Secession to Reconstruction*. Washington, DC: National Geographic, 2006.

Lincoln, Abraham. Abraham Lincoln Papers at the Library of Congress. American Memory. www.memory.loc.gov/ammem/alhtml/malhome.html.

Longstreet, James. *From Manassas to Appomattox: Memoirs of the Civil War in America*. Philadelphia: J. B. Lippincott, 1896.

———. "Our March Against Pope." In *Battles and Leaders of the Civil War: Being for the Most Part Contributions of Union and Confederate Officers*. Vol. 2. New York: Century Co., 1888.

Lowe, Thaddeus S. C. "The Balloons with the Army of the Potomac." In *The Photographic History of the Civil War in Ten Volumes*. Vol. 8. Edited by Francis Trevelyan Miller. New York: Review of Reviews, 1911.

———. *Memoirs of Thaddeus S. C. Lowe, Chief of the Aeronautic Corps of the Army of the United States During the Civil War: My Balloons in Peace and War*. Edited by Michael Jaeger and Carol Lauritzen. Lewiston, NY: Edwin Mellen Press, 2004.

———. "Observation Balloons in the Battle of Fair Oaks." *American Review of Reviews*, February 1911, 186–190.

———. Papers. Archives of the Institute of Aerospace Sciences, 1783–1962. Manuscript Division, Library of Congress, Washington, DC.

———. "T. S. C. Lowe's Official Report." In U.S. War Department. *The War of the Rebellion: A Compilation of the Official Records of the Union and Confederate Armies*. Series 3, Vol. 3. Washington, DC: Government Printing Office, 1899, 252–319.

McClellan, George B. *The Civil War Papers of George B. McClellan: Selected Correspondence, 1860–1865*. Edited by Stephen W. Sears. New York: Ticknor and Fields, 1989.

———. *McClellan's Own Story: The War for the Union, the Soldiers Who Fought It, the Civilians Who Directed It and His Relations to It and Them*. New York: Charles L. Webster, 1887.

McElfresh, Earl B. "Blinded Giant: The Role of Maps in Robert E. Lee's Gettysburg Campaign." *Mercator's World*, May–June 2000, 30–37.

———. "Make Straight His Path: Mapmaking in the Civil War." *Civil War Times Illustrated*, June 2007, 36–43.

———. *Maps and Mapmakers of the Civil War*. New York: Harry N. Abrams, 1999.

McPherson, James M. *Battle Cry of Freedom: The Civil War Era*. New York: Oxford University Press, 1998.

———. *Ordeal by Fire: The Civil War and Reconstruction*. 3rd ed. New York: McGraw-Hill, 2001.

# BIBLIOGRAPHY

Milbank, Jeremiah, Jr. *The First Century of Flight in America: An Introductory Survey*. Princeton, NJ: Princeton University Press, 1943.

Nevins, Allan. *Hamilton Fish: The Inner History of the Grant Administration*. New York: Dodd, Mead, 1936.

*New York Times*, "The Great Balloon," October 25, 1859.

*New York Times*, "News of the Day," September 9, 1861.

*New York Times*, "The Order Onward!", March 17, 1862.

Nisbet, Eugenius Aristides. Papers. Special Collections Library, Duke University, Durham, NC.

O'Brien, John Emmet. *Telegraphing in Battle: Reminiscences of the Civil War*. Scranton, PA: Raeder Press, 1910.

O'Reilly, Francis Augustin. *The Fredericksburg Campaign: Winter War on the Rappahannock*. Baton Rouge: Louisiana State University Press, 2003.

Pfanz, Donald C. *War So Terrible: A Popular History of the Battle of Fredericksburg*. Richmond, VA: Page One History Publications, 2003.

Poindexter, John F. Papers. Special Collections Library, Duke University, Durham, NC.

Porter, Fitz John. "Hanover Court House and Gaines's Mill." In *Battles and Leaders of the Civil War: Being for the Most Part Contributions of Union and Confederate Officers*. Vol. 2. New York: Century Co., 1888.

Rable, George C. *Fredericksburg! Fredericksburg!* Chapel Hill: University of North Carolina Press, 2002.

Rolt, L. T. C. *The Aeronauts: A History of Ballooning, 1783–1903*. London: Longmans, Green, 1966.

Sandburg, Carl. *Abraham Lincoln: The War Years in Four Volumes*. Vol. 1. New York: Harcourt Brace, 1939.

Scharf, Jonathan Thomas. *The Personal Memoirs of Jonathan Thomas Scharf of the First Maryland Artillery*. Edited by Tom Kelley. Baltimore: Butternut and Blue, 1992.

Sears, Stephen W. *George B. McClellan: The Young Napoleon*. New York: Ticknor and Fields, 1988.

———. *To the Gates of Richmond: The Peninsula Campaign*. New York: Ticknor and Fields, 1992.

Seims, Charles. *Mount Lowe: The Railway in the Clouds*. San Marino, CA: Golden West Books, 1976.

Sneden, Private Robert Knox. *Eye of the Storm: A Civil War Odyssey*. Edited by Charles F. Bryan, Jr., and Nelson D. Lankford. New York: Free Press, 2000.

Squires, J. Duane. "Aeronautics in the Civil War." *The American Historical Review*, July 1937, 652–669.

Stackpole, Edward J. *Drama on the Rappahannock: The Fredericksburg Campaign*. Harrisburg, PA: Military Service Publishing, 1957.

# BIBLIOGRAPHY

Stanchak, John E., ed. *Leslie's Illustrated Civil War*. Jackson: University Press of Mississippi, 1992.

Steiner, Paul E. *Disease in the Civil War: Natural Biological Warfare in 1861–1865*. Springfield, IL: Charles C. Thomas, 1968.

Stevens, Benjamin C. Papers. Special Collections Library, Duke University, Durham, NC.

Styple, William B., ed. *Writing and Fighting the Civil War: Soldier Correspondence to the New York Sunday Mercury*. Kearny, NJ: Belle Grove Publishing, 2004.

Thompson, S. Millett. *Thirteenth Regiment of New Hampshire Volunteer Infantry in the War of the Rebellion, 1861–1865: A Diary Covering Three Years and a Day*. Boston: Houghton Mifflin, 1888.

Townsend, George Alfred. *Rustics in Rebellion: A Yankee Reporter on the Road to Richmond, 1861–65*. Chapel Hill: University of North Carolina Press, 1950.

Tufts, William. Diary. Richmond National Battlefield Park, Richmond, VA.

University of Richmond. *Richmond Daily Dispatch, 1860–1865*. dlxs.richmond.edu/d/ddr.

U.S. War Department. *The War of the Rebellion: A Compilation of the Official Records of the Union and Confederate Armies*. Series 1, Vols. 5, 10, 11, and 25; Series 2, Vol. 2; Series 3, Vol. 3. Washington, DC: Government Printing Office, 1880–1901.

Wise, John. *A System of Aeronautics*. Philadelphia: Joseph A. Speel, 1850.

———. *Through the Air: A Narrative of Forty Years' Experience as an Aeronaut*. New York: Arno Press, 1972. Reprint of 1873 edition.

Zeller, Bob. *The Blue and Gray in Black and White: A History of Civil War Photography*. Westport, CT: Praeger, 2005.

# FOR MORE INFORMATION*

In addition to the resources listed in the bibliography, readers may be interested in the following:

### ON THADDEUS LOWE

Professor Thaddeus Lowe.
www.thaddeuslowe.name.
    Contains photographs, articles, and other resources. Web site is maintained by one of Lowe's descendants.

Karr, Kathleen. *Spy in the Sky*. New York: Hyperion Books for Children, 1997.
    Novel for young readers about a ten-year-old orphan who becomes Thaddeus Lowe's assistant.

Poleskie, Stephen. *The Balloonist: The Story of T. S. C. Lowe—Inventor, Scientist, Magician, and Father of the U.S. Air Force*. Savannah, GA: Frederic C. Beil, 2007.
    Novel for teens and adults about Lowe's life.

### ON BALLOONING

*History Detectives*.
www.pbs.org/opb/historydetectives.
    View video and read transcripts from PBS's *History Detectives* episodes about Civil War balloons, war balloons, and Civil War photography.

*Balloon Race Around the World. Nova* Online.
www.pbs.org/wgbh/nova/balloon/.
    Learn about the race to circle the world in a balloon. Read the transcript of the *Nova* broadcast "Danger in the Jet Stream." Take a virtual balloon flight. Site contains information about the history and science of ballooning and links to ballooning Web sites.

Albuquerque International Balloon Fiesta.
www.balloonfiesta.com.
    Web site for the world's largest annual balloon gathering. See the "gas balloons" section to learn how modern balloons work.

### ON THE CIVIL WAR

*The Civil War: A Film by Ken Burns*.
www.pbs.org/civilwar/.
    PBS site for the film contains video clips, photographs, information about the war, and lists of Civil War books and Web sites.

Civil War Maps. American Memory, Library of Congress.
www.memory.loc.gov/ammem/collections/civil_war_maps/.
    View approximately three thousand Civil War maps that show battlefields, attack plans, troop movements, and fortifications.

*Web sites active at time of publication

# FOR MORE INFORMATION

Selected Civil War Photographs Collection. American Memory, Library of Congress. www.memory.loc.gov/ammem/cwphtml.

A searchable collection of more than a thousand images. Includes information about the photographs and a Civil War timeline.

CivilWar@Smithsonian. National Portrait Gallery, Smithsonian Institution. www.civilwar.si.edu.

The Smithsonian's online collection of Civil War portraits, photographs, and artifacts. Site also includes a timeline as well as lists of other resources about Lincoln, Civil War leaders and soldiers, and weapons.

Kagan, Neil, ed. *Eyewitness to the Civil War: The Complete History from Secession to Reconstruction.* Washington, DC: National Geographic, 2006.

An illustrated overview of the Civil War with archival photographs, maps, a timeline, and an extensive list of books for further reading.

McPherson, James M. *The Illustrated Battle Cry of Freedom: The Civil War Era.* New York: Oxford University Press, 2003.

The illustrated edition of the Pulitzer Prize–winning history of the Civil War. Contains photographs, maps, cartoons, and illustrations from newspapers of the time.

Miller, William J., and Brian C. Pohanka. *An Illustrated History of the Civil War: Images of an American Tragedy.* Alexandria, VA: Time-Life Books, 2000.

Covers the people, battles, and events of the Civil War using archival photographs, maps, and engravings.

## PLACES TO VISIT

**Smithsonian National Air and Space Museum**, Washington, D.C. www.nasm.si.edu.

See the exhibits about Thaddeus Lowe, the Civil War spy balloons, and balloon flight throughout history.

**Richmond National Battlefield Park**, Richmond, Virginia. www.nps.gov/rich/.

Find out more about the Peninsula Campaign of 1862, during which both sides of the conflict used surveillance balloons. Visit museums and battlefield sites managed by the National Park Service.

**Fredericksburg and Spotsylvania County National Military Park**, Fredericksburg, Virginia. www.nps.gov/frsp/.

Learn about the battles of Fredericksburg and Chancellorsville at the visitor centers and battlefield walking trails.

# INDEX

Page numbers in **boldface** refer to
photographs and captions.

# INDEX

# PICTURE CREDITS

Private Collection, Courtesy of **Lance Ferm**: 3, 13 (bottom left and right), 41, 88, 91.

Courtesy of **R. A. Jarrow**: 16.

**Library of Congress, American Memory, The Abraham Lincoln Papers**: 27.

**Library of Congress, Manuscript Division**, American Institute of Aeronautics and Astronautics Collection: 13 (top), 17, 18, 19, 33, 34, 43, 44, 52, 85, 87.

**Library of Congress, Prints and Photographs Division**, Civil War Photographs Collection, LC-B11-2348: 8; LC-USZ62-17468: 10; Tissandier Collection, LC-USZ61-1722: 12; LC-USZ62-11594: 14; LC-USZ62-42864: 15; LC-USZC2-2663: 20; Landauer Collection, LC-USZ62-65649: 23; Brady-Handy Photograph Collection, LC-BH824-4499: 24; LC-B8184-4196: 25; LC-USZ62-71022: 26; Civil War Photographs Collection, LC-B815-254: 28; Meserve Collection, LC-USZ62-7990: 30; Civil War Photographs Collection, LC-B811-2310: 32; LC-USZ62-5653: 35; Civil War Photographs Collection, LC-B813-1765: 38; LC-USZ62-56907: 45; LC-USZ62-82807: 48; Civil War Photographs Collection, LC-B811-334: 49; Brady-Handy Photograph Collection, LC-BH82-3817: 51; Civil War Photographs Collection, LC-USZC4-7995: 53; LC-USZ62-109737: 55; Civil War Photographs Collection, LC-USZ62-68172: 57; Brady-Handy Photograph Collection, LC-BH832-2016: 58; LC-USZ62-64161: 64; LC-USZ62-3277: 65; Civil War Photographs Collection, LC-B811-2349: 66; Civil War Photographs Collection, LC-B8171-7383: 67; Civil War Photographs Collection, LC-BH831-565: 71; Civil War Photographs Collection, LC-B815-491: 73; Civil War Photographs Collection LC-B813-1625: 75; LC-B8184-10331: 76; LC-USZ62-139: 77; Civil War Photographs Collection, LC-B817-7927: 78; Civil War Drawing Collection, LC-USZ62-79222: 79; Civil War Photographs Collection, LC-B815-678: 80; Civil War Photographs Collection, LC-B813-6385: 81; Landauer Collection, LC-USZ62-42856: 82; LC-USZ62-5453: 84; Detroit Publishing Company Photograph Collection, LC-USZ62-118093: 89; Tissandier Collection, LC-DIG-ppmsca-02639: 90.

**National Archives and Records Administration (NARA)**, Still Picture Branch: 21 (top), 29 (left and right), 40, 42, 47, 59, 63, 69, 72.

From **E. P. Porter**, *Military Memoirs of a Confederate: A Critical Narrative*. New York: Charles Scribner's Sons, 1907: 61.

**Wikimedia Commons**, Doubleeagleii: 21 (bottom); Portsmouth,_NH_-_Fitz_John_Porter_panel_3: 54.

# Acknowledgments

I appreciate the help of the following experts who graciously shared their knowledge:

Tom Crouch, senior curator of the Aeronautics Division, Smithsonian Institution National Air and Space Museum, who answered questions and reviewed my manuscript;

Robert E. L. Krick, historian at the Richmond National Battlefield Park and the Maggie L. Walker National Historic Site, who provided a Yankee soldier's unpublished diary and checked my manuscript; Mike Gorman, Susie Sernaker, and Klydie Thomas from the National Park Service at Richmond, who supplied information about the Peninsula Campaign;

Donald Pfanz, historian at the Fredericksburg and Spotsylvania County Battlefields National Military Park, who read over my chapter on the battles of Fredericksburg and Chancellorsville;

 D. P. Newton, curator of the White Oak Civil War Museum, Falmouth, Virginia, for his knowledge of the Union army camps near Fredericksburg;

Lowe family members Lance Ferm and Terry D. Lowe for their help with Thaddeus Lowe's genealogy;

Earl McElfresh of McElfresh Map Company, an expert on Civil War maps;

Maureen and Chris Lynch for their knowledge of nineteenth-century balloon making;

Carroll and Miriam Teitsworth of Liberty Balloon Company for demonstrating the operation of a hot air balloon and then taking me up in one.

Thanks to the staffs at the Library of Congress Manuscript Reading Room and the Duke University Rare Book, Manuscript, and Special Collections Library.

In gathering photographs for this book, I had the assistance of Bob Zeller, president of the Center for Civil War Photography, who provided information about images and checked captions; Lance Ferm, who generously shared his personal family photographs; Joe McCary of Photo Response Studio; and the staffs of the Library of Congress Photo Duplication Services, the Still Picture Reference Team at the National Archives and Records Administration, and the Smithsonian Institution National Air and Space Museum Archives.

For their help in turning my manuscript into this book, I thank Jeryl Genschow, Jeff George, and Joan Hyman.

Special thanks go to Carolyn P. Yoder for her editorial guidance, encouragement, and enthusiasm for history.

—G.J.